The radio crac... I have learned much about you, *Phü Nhãm*, killer, and I believe it is time that we meet. May I introduce myself? My name is Ngu Diem Han. We are in the same line of work, so to speak.''

''I know a little bit about you, too.'' Rossen's voice was cold and steady. ''You're supposed to be the Cong's number-one shooter.''

Ngu had a pleasant, tinkling laugh. ''I am pleased that you have heard of me. It will make things easier for you to understand. Now, do not interrupt me. This is what I propose. I believe we are much the same; we have no use for politicians or abstract social ideologies. We deal in the greatest of truths—the giving and taking of life.

''I want you to come to me . . .''

Rossen, the Ice Man, the killer, *Phü Nhãm*, listened and began to plan.

PHÜ NHÃM

Barry Sadler

PHÜ NHÃM

TOR

A TOM DOHERTY ASSOCIATES BOOK

PHÜ NHÂM

A TOR Book

Published by Tom Doherty Associates
8-10 West 36th Street
New York, N.Y. 10018

First TOR printing: June 1984

ISBN: 58825-8
CAN. ED. 58826-6

Printed in the United States of America

PROLOGUE

The face looking back at him from the fogged mirror didn't belong to anyone he knew. The eyes had a different quality to them, their once deep blue having faded with time into a pale shade of mist. Now there was something distant in them, alone. The face was vaguely familiar. The jaw line was sharper than he remembered and the cheeks more pronounced. The lips had lost what humor they'd once held. His face had become that of a predator, someone—something—who had to kill to live. And, like all predators, he knew that the time would come when he would be the hunted.

He ran his hands over his eyes to hide the reflection. He stopped, held his hand out in front of him, fingers spread wide. They trembled. . . .

Jim Rossen focused his eyes on the shaking fingers. He concentrated, took a deep breath, held it, then slowly let it out, bending his trigger finger as if taking up the slack on a rifle. The trembling stopped. Habit had taken over. The digits were doing what they knew best.

Lowering his head, he sat back down on the edge of his bed, ignoring the damp spot under him, a remnant of dreams and night sweat. Naked, he sat, head held tight between his hands. The room was lit only by the dull glow of a single, greasy, bare 60-watt bulb in a cheap porcelain socket overhead that gave the dingy quarters the stark look of a cell—and Rossen the look of one held captive by his own mind and fears.

From the street outside he could hear hawkers still crying out for someone to buy their wares. Some sold fish from the Malay Sea; others, women or drugs. In Singapore everything was for sale, even life. Through the decaying bamboo blinds, which tried, unsuccessfully, to keep the outside world away, a thin breeze tried to enter into the heaviness of the room. The breeze, the last remnant of a tropical storm, had come far that night, drifting from across the Sulu Sea to try and cool the night. But it had failed; now it only served to move the sweltering heat of Asia around in slow waves and rustled the wind chimes on the Buddhist temple near the Telok Basin.

Rossen's flesh rippled with a sweaty chill that caused the delicate skin under the rib cage to tighten, accenting the puckered, heavier tissue that built up in round, smooth, reddish mounds where copper-nosed bullets had entered and passed through. These were still fresh wounds. In time they would fade to match the paler shade of the other scars on his body. His medals, his history. They were easy to see, to identify. Less obvious were the wounds in his mind. He knew them, but only he. He also knew what he needed to put away the dreams and fears that rode his sleep—dreams that caused the tremor in his hands and the sour sweat to drain from his pores. He knew what he needed, and Singapore would give it to him.

He checked his watch, a Seiko with an olive-drab band. 0133 hours. Before putting on the cheap, white cotton shirt he'd bought earlier, he wiped his body down with a thin, threadbare towel that didn't have enough material left in it to soak up all the moisture on his body. Khaki pants, over combat boots that hadn't seen a real shine in weeks, completed his ensemble. He looked like any other GI on R&R. If he'd been wearing a two-hundred-dollar Hong Kong suit, he would still have stood out in a crowd, easy to spot as a soldier. The short-cropped, sandy hair, with a touch of premature grey starting at the temples, rested on his head like a skull cap. Just the way he moved—with a wariness that watched every shadow, every car or motor scooter; his body tensed, ready to jump—made it easy to see he was fresh from Vietnam.

He closed the door to his room behind him, leaving the light on. He didn't like coming back to a dark room. He left his shirt tails out of his waistband, as many did in the tropics. Most felt that it let the skin breathe a bit better. It also served to keep the .380 Walther PPK in his belt concealed and easy to reach.

The Chinese desk clerk watched him as he left to go onto the streets and wondered why this American wasn't at one of the hotels that catered to their trade—the Western-style places where they could get hamburgers and hot dogs and sleep in rooms that Holiday Inn would approve of.

Rossen didn't want that. He was where he needed to be, where he was the most comfortable. The antiseptic rooms of the Western hotels offended him with their cleanliness, their stiff, scratchy sheets and their trained staff members who smiled with airline-stewardess grins at every piece of shit that came through their doors and could pay the price of a room.

No! It was better for him here in the Chinese section of town. He had no need or desire for the new world of boring, sterile Western hotels or that remnant of Britain's colonial empire, Raffles. This was where he belonged—with the rich smell of life and death.

Stepping out into the street, he paused, lit a smoke and looked from right to left taking in everything in sight—the texture of the streets, the cobblestones laid two hundred years before and constantly damp from the mist that came from the sea; lamps around which squadrons of night moths hovered and circled, waiting to be attacked by streaking shadows that plunged like dive bombers among the flying insects, flickered, then were gone.

A bat carried off another moth to eat.

The sea seemed to touch everything; the air was heavy with it. Small beads of moisture had already started to collect on the fine hairs on his arms and the back of his hands. His six-foot-two frame dwarfed the smaller Asians as he passed among them. Small men who had never eaten a steak in their lives moved out of the way of the giant. Conical hats of woven straw were held to their heads by chin bands of once bright cloth. They went about the daily effort of trying to survive one more night. In doorways aged crones smoked home-grown and cured tobacco rolled in green leaves and spat eternally through teeth blackened by a lifetime of chewing betel nut. From some doorways younger eyes, eyes gazing from smooth, golden-skinned faces framed by thick, flowing hair of ebony, also watched the broad back of the man and were tempted to call to him, to offer him dreams and pleasures he had never known. All for the price of a meal or a carton of Salem cigarettes.

Survival! Nowhere in the world except the Orient is the word truly understood. Children learn the rules by the time they are able to walk. There is no good or evil— there is only survival. He knew that it would not be long before the beautiful oval faces of the Malay and Chinese girls would grow old and their beauty fade and, before they were thirty, leave them like the crones who chewed their betel nut and spat blood-red juice on the damp stones of the streets. If they did not save enough money to provide themselves with a dowry, they would be reduced every season to less desirable haunts and less money, until, diseased and broken, they sat and chewed the betel nut and its leaves and lived on fantasies with the oth-

ers like them. But even then they would
somehow survive.

He understood that. It was the only rule
one truly needed. All the rest merely served
to make life complicated. He was a survivor
because he knew what he was and accepted
it. The ones who lost were those who questioned themselves and their motives. He had
questions but he kept them away, knowing
how dangerous they were.

It had taken much longer to learn that
truth: To survive, be what you are. People
had tried to make him into different things
over the years, and he had tried to be what
they wanted, but it never worked. All it
achieved was to make those who cared for
him change their feelings from love to hate
because he couldn't live by their rules and
illusions. He knew what he was. He didn't
belong with those who worked all their lives
so they could sit in a sunny spot and wait
to die.

A peasant with a load of birds in cages tied
to a bicycle brushed by him. The Malay
smiled at him with wrinkled eyes and went
on disappearing into the night, taking his
birds to market.

Ahead of him a sign in English beckoned:
"BEER." He had been there before. It was
one of those tiny, narrow places where the
bar ran the full length of the single room,

where a half-dozen tables were occupied by blank-faced girls who hustled foreign sailors and soldiers for drinks. Though he'd never been *in* the place, he knew it well. Knew that when he entered the doors, eyes would check him over. Then, for a moment, the eyes would light up and come to life. The doll-like girls would look at each other, come to some kind of unspoken agreement about who was to have first crack at him. Once he'd made his selection, the other eyes would go blank again as they waited for the next face to come in.

Rossen paused before entering the smoked-glass single door. When he did push it open to go inside, it was with the slow, overly deliberate steps of one who had had too much to drink. He ignored the glances from the girls as he went to the bar and ordered a double shot of scotch from the fat amah from Tonkin who ran the bar. And the girls. He tossed the drink down neat, wiped his mouth with the back of his hand, and ordered another.

One of the bar girls, an import from Kuala Lumpur, slid up next to him. Her eyes were dark almonds, set wide in an oval face that could have graced many of the carvings he'd seen on Hindu temples. It was a face that was timeless. The smile was automatic, her eyes bright and moist from eating opium.

He bought her a drink. What they called in Nam "Saigon Tea." That was all it was, tea with just enough whiskey in it to give it a little odor in case a suspicious John wanted to smell to make sure he was paying for a real drink.

He looked around the bar. Two Irish sailors off a freighter with Panamanian registry sat at one table. Each of them had one of the bar dolls sitting on his lap. At the rear of the bar he saw what he was looking for. Two men in their twenties who looked too clean, too well-fed, their hair slicked back with oil. The fingernails on the left hands had grown so long the nails on their little fingers had begun to curve, turning into hooks designed to rip out an eye. They probably took Kung Fu lessons three times a week. He avoided any direct eye contact with them; he'd seen enough. The rest of the patrons in the club didn't interest him.

Muttering drunkenly, he ignored the pleading of the Malay girl to go out the back door and across the alley to where she had a room. He paid for his drinks from a roll of green American currency. Four months' pay. Tossing a ten on the bar, he half-stumbled back out the door and waited a moment.

He knew what was taking place inside. The girl had told the two young men and right now they were deciding if he was worth going after. Moving across the street, he stopped in front of a window, not noticing or caring what was inside the shop, and used the window as a mirror. The two men came out. They spotted him, but this was not the place for what they had planned—it was too light and there were a few police patrols that came by at irregular times.

Rossen stumbled off. He'd give them what they sought. He turned the corner, taking him closer to the Telok Basin and the waterfront two blocks away from the dimly lit section where the club waited like a thin, hungry spider for its next victim. He kept up his charade. He walked with his head lowered, swinging loose on his shoulders. His feet seemed to move by themselves, uncertain of just when to take the next step. He moved farther into the dark streets, not looking to right or left. The smell from the gutters on each side of the dank street almost sickened him. From behind shuttered windows he heard a baby's cry and the universal soothing sounds of a mother comforting her child.

He moved on. He could hear footsteps behind him. One of them was wearing hard leather heels that clicked with authority and confidence. The smell of the sea was strong, and mixed with that of oil, garbage and fish. The wind had shifted, taking the mist back out to the open waters. There was no one on the streets alongside the narrow road leading to the docks. They would do it soon.

He picked his spot, resting his shoulder against a weathered concrete statue of Buddha. There were street lights on either side of him about a half block away. The Walther PPK pinched the tender skin near his groin. To one side he heard thin, shuffling sounds; on the other, the clicking of the leather heels. They were splitting up to come at him from two directions. His left leg suddenly fell out from under him as he drunkenly lurched, bent over, grabbed the Buddha, and came back up to his feet. This time the PPK was by his side—out of sight in his hand, safety off, the hammer back.

The two Chinese looked at each other and smiled. This was going to be easy meat. The drunken fool was ready to pass out. They moved closer, each of them with a narrow-bladed Filipino flip-knife in his hand. They held the blades point-down by their sides, cutting edges up, as they closed to within ten feet. Rossen straightened completely, the Walther rising with him, the bore pointed straight at the face of the man to his left. There was no hesitation. His finger had already taken in the slack on the trigger and there was less than a half-pound of pull left to release the sear. The small weapon bucked once in his hand and the Chinese's right eye exploded as the .380 round passed through it into his brain, and splintered. The man dropped as though his legs had suddenly been amputated and there wasn't anything to keep his body up. The dead man's friend froze as the bore of the pistol swung to him. The flip-knife dropped from his fingers to the cobblestones. His mouth suddenly went foul, burning with the sour taste of bile. He raised his hands in front of him, as if they could ward off the bullet and prevent the round from reaching him.

Rossen felt no regret, no sense of foul play. They had come after him. If they had chosen to stay in the bar, nothing would have happened. This night was of their making, and if they were going to be big game hunters, then they shouldn't complain if their prey turned on them. Still, he felt that perhaps he should be a bit more sporting. He motioned with his pistol to his right, toward the street light.

"Try for it."

Eyes wild with fear, the Chinese looked at the face of the man in front of him and knew that he meant it. He had a chance. The small pistol in the American's hand wasn't designed for long-range shooting. If he could reach the light, he'd be out of range.

"I'll count to four. If you're still here, I'll kill you where you stand. *One!*"

The Chinese broke for it and ran for the light. Once there he would be only two steps away from safety by making the corner which would take him out of sight.

"Two." He stumbled, slipping on the wet cobblestones.

"Three." He opened his mouth to breathe, regained his feet, tears flowing down his face. He was almost to the light, felt the glow of the lamp on his face. He was almost there.

"Four." He had reached the light. One more step and he was safe. The back of his head erupted. Brain tissue and bone splinters flew out of what had been his face. His legs kept trying to run; they didn't know yet that he was dead.

Then the message from the jellied brain reached them.

Rossen walked over to the body and examined the effect that the mercury-cored bullets had on human flesh. Then, putting the pistol back in his waistband, he dragged both bodies by the heels to where he could shove them off a ramp and into the basin. The tide was beginning to go; they wouldn't be back until dawn. If the sharks didn't get them—if they did, the two dead punks would disappear. He wasn't concerned about the police. To them, this would be just another gangland killing, part of the running battle between the Chinese colony and the Malays, which had become a way of life on the waterfront area of Singapore. Even if the police did investigate the killings, they'd find nothing. He'd be on a plane for Saigon by 0900 hours. Just another GI on his way back to the war.

He felt better. Holding his hands in front of his face, he looked at them. Steady as a rock. . . . More like the code name give him by S2.

The Ice Man. . . .

PART ONE

Chapter One

Singapore seemed as far away as the States. It was amazing how rapidly you slipped back into familiar patterns as though the past days had never existed.

Around Rossen and the others mosquitoes hummed, riding on thin waves of heavy morning air. It was time to bug out before they got their ass. ate up either by the damned bugs or by the Cong.

He watched Tomanaga out of the corner of his eye. The nisei showed no expression or sign of worry on his face. It was as steady and unconcerned as if they'd been on a target range stateside. His eyes were red, itching from the hours of having to constantly scope out the area. Rubbing them with the

back of his hand, he went back to watching
the Hardball—the raised trail that ran between the rice paddies. He couldn't hear
them, but knew that swarms of tiny, black,
sucking, stinging flies were gathering in
clouds around the bodies lying there. Once
more he wondered about Tomanaga. The
man was as good a partner as he could
have asked for. He wondered if Tomanaga
was ever as scared as he was, or did his
Japanese background change his viewpoints?

Tomanaga nudged Rossen on the elbow.
A thin, erratic drone was coming close. It
was the "Cavalry" coming to the rescue and
about damned time.

Tomanaga was ready to leave too. This
waiting-around shit was getting on his
nerves. He didn't know how Rossen could
just lie there for days without ever making
a sign that it was bothering him. Maybe he
had some Indian blood in him. They were
supposed to be good at this kind of thing.

Rossen gave one last scope of the area.
Nothing moved. Good!

"Okay, let's get ready to move out."
Tomanaga and the four men of his security
team would have cheered if their throats
hadn't been so tightly gripped by fear.

Just to their rear, by a stand of nipa palms,
the helicopters began to unload their car-
gos of men. One full company from the 7th.

Once they had the full unit on the deck, he and Tomanaga would go with them out to the Hardball and search the bodies of the dead VC. Once that was done, their job would be over. Now all they wanted was out.

Tomanaga was on the radio talking to the flight leader.

"Keep your eyes open up there. Tell those grunts on the ground we're coming out and not to get trigger-happy if they see a gook in cammies, 'cause that'll be me!"

A laugh crackled back out of the receiver. "Is that you, Tomanaga?"

Tomanaga barked back. "Who the hell did you think it was? Toshiro Mifune?"

The laugh continued. "This is Sam, and you still owe me ten bucks, sucker. If I promise to get you out alive, are you going to pay me?"

"Listen to me, you blackmailing shit. If you don't get us out, I'm going to tell Rossen that you're a legitimate target."

Lieutenant Samuel Benson had no desire to tempt fate with that remote possibility.

"Don't get your chopsticks in an uproar. Tell the Ice Man we're ready to take you out."

Major Hernandez, the G2, was called in for the after-action report. He was a tall, thin man with sharp features that had Castile written all over them. Rossen thought he looked like some portraits he'd once seen in a book about Spanish grandees; all he needed was the spade beard and mustache.

"Good day, Colonel Sergeant Rossen. How did it go?"

Rossen pointed to the bag on the desk containing the documents and papers he'd taken off the bodies. Hernandez gave them a cursory once-over, but he couldn't tell much. He'd have to have them translated later, though he had a suspicion of what they contained—lists of the names of Viet Cong leaders in the villages around the area and the number of guerrillas they could muster.

Rossen approved of the G2 officer; he wasn't overly filled with bullshit and tried to do a good job. Tomlin wasn't so fond of him, but he knew the Major did most of the work that was credited to him and he couldn't do without his brain.

Hernandez knew his value to Tomlin, but didn't care who got the credit as along as the job was done. Taking a chair, he leaned back without waiting for Tomlin to give permission and began.

"Okay, Sarge, take it from the top, beginning at the insertion."

Rossen closed his eyes to put his thoughts in focus and began.

"The insertion was made with no problems. As you know, we went in on two Loaches so that they could get out fast if any shit started. Once on the deck, me and Tomanaga, along with our security team, moved out. We had set down at dusk, about four or five clicks from the target area. The area was pretty heavily covered with thickets and marsh, so it took longer than we planned to cover the four or five clicks. By the time we reached the target area, it was about an hour to light.

"We took up a partial position till it got light enough to get a good look at the terrain. We were in an area where there was a large creek lined with a lot of nipa palms and bamboo and brush bordering several large rice paddies.

"Within five or six hundred meters of the site we were in at that time, there was another heavily wooded area to our rear. A single Hardball crossed almost parallel to us, so we looked around for a good place to set up. We found a sort of low-lying area where we could get good places to lay up for prone shooting and still see over the other rice dikes. If the info you gave was right, then the targets we were waiting for would more than likely be coming down this Hardball. It was the only dry ground leading straight through the paddies.

"I put one of the security team men on an out area where he could keep track of what was going on and Tomanaga out on the other side so that we'd have a minor perimeter set up. Then we went to work building a blind, taking our cuttings, as always, from an area a couple of hundred meters off where it was not likely that any Dinks would enter. We spent the day staying alert, but I gave everyone a chance to rest when it was possible. With half of us on watch and half asleep.

"We settled in for the night at about 1800 or so and had no contacts. We did see one who might have been a VC moving around, but we let him go. We spent that night with no further contacts.

"Before dawn we checked our area again, made sure no Dinks were in the vicinity, then redid our blinds, making sure that they were properly placed. Then I sent Sergeant Tomanaga and one of the security team men out on their bellies to the Hardball and had them check out our positions from the enemy's point of view. It was all right. Even knowing where we were, Tommy couldn't see any of us, so we knew we were pretty well set there."

The report on the operation sounded flat,

dry, without emotions, as though it were
being read from a textbook. It was Hernandez who had given him the code name "Ice
Man," but he wasn't always cold. Only when
he was actually working did most feelings
leave and he became one with his weapon.
There was no way for him to tell them of
the feelings he had as he lay there through
the first night, guts jerking at every noise or
cry of a night bird. That first day and night
had gone by with time weighing on his
shoulders like a heated anvil. Cold C rations for chow sat in the gut like lumps of
lead, and you hated to eat because sooner
or later it was going to have to come out. It
wasn't very dignified to squat and shit in
your own position, then cover it up like a
dog. Even then the smell never seemed to
go away, though you knew it was in your
mind.

It took control, discipline; you had to force
yourself to be able to stay like that for
long periods of time. He and Tomanaga had
done it a hundred times and it was still
hard. You never got used to it. He knew it
was a lot worse for the security team. They
weren't trained or really prepared for this
kind of work. He knew the terror that a
man's imagination can create for him, knew
the pressure of maintaining absolute silence
and, above all, of staying absolutely still.

Remember when you used to go hunting? Nine times out of ten it was the movement of the animal that gave it away.

So: Don't move! Don't talk! Don't make the smallest sound! Just because you can't see them doesn't mean the VC aren't close by. Or that one you can't see won't look your way for a just a second and see a tiny movement in the brush when there is no wind to cause it, and if he does, you'll die!

Hernandez listened to Rossen's report. He knew he was only getting the bare bones. Colonel Tomlin didn't notice, but Hernandez saw the pulse in Rossen's temple beat stronger, faster, as he told his story.

As for Rossen, he relived every second again.

The second night started quiet again. The moon was quite good—full, round and silver, nearly bright enough to read by. At 2140 hours he saw four Viets moving about, but he let them go. They were just traveling on the Hardballs and he couldn't see any weapons on them. Nerves were getting a bit tight, but they began to get a good moon. Then came the water, rising up over the dikes to where they lay in their blinds. Inch by inch it creeped up to them. There was no way to keep dry. The water stopped rising when it reached their bellies. Just enough to keep them soaked and miserable for the rest of

the night. He and Tomanaga did their best
to keep their weapons from getting wet.
Water didn't go well with the delicate lenses
of their scopes.

He didn't know if a high tide from the sea
had come in or if it had rained upriver. The
wet and cold was bad enough, but the rising water also brought something else with
it—leeches. Black and brown, slender strands
of blood-sucking tissue swelled as as they
fed, then, when fully sated, dropped off their
victims to wait for the next time they needed
to feed, which could be weeks or even
months. Rossen first knew he had them when
he felt one crawling on his face right at the
corner of his mouth. He pulled it off before
it had a chance to get a good grip.

Nudging Tomanaga, he whispered, "We
got company."

Tomanaga at first thought he meant Dinks
were coming down the Hardball; then he
saw the squiggly thing between Rossen's
wet, dirty fingers.

"Aw, shit!" Tomanaga hissed between his
teeth, and started checking himself over.

It would have been best if they'd been
able to light a cigarette and burn them off
or put salt on them. But they had neither,
and even if they'd had any smokes with
them, Rossen wouldn't have let them light
up. They'd just have to pull them off by

hand and have the bites treated later when they got back.

Two hours before dawn the waters receded, draining slowly back into the river and the paddies.

It was daylight before they got the last of the creatures off them. Rossen and Tomanaga took turns watching the Hardball as the others stripped naked to get at the leeches, which had managed to find openings in their fatigues and were sucking happily away at legs, stomachs and groins. Rossen knew the security team was having the same problems when he heard a muted curse. He snapped his fingers! The guilty party looked at him. Rossen pointed his finger straight between the man's eyes and shook his head side-to-side slowly, deliberately. The trooper got the message. Rossen didn't care if the leeches ate his family jewels off. There would be no noise.

The next day was a repeat. He thought about moving, but to where? This was still the best route to take through the paddies. If a big shot was coming this way, he'd probably be pretty much like the American brass and not want to have to wade five miles through knee-deep muck.

Hernandez interrupted him on a small point. "Have you and the others had the leech bites looked at yet? Those can get infected pretty easily."

Wiping his forehead with the dirty sleeve of his camouflage jacket, as it had suddenly got much warmer in the confines of the Colonel's office, Rossen nodded in the affirmative. "Yes, sir. Tomanaga and the others are at the dispensary now. I'll go as soon as we finish the de-briefing."

Tomlin was anxious to get the boring bull-shit over with. He had a date for drinks with the PIO officer in less than an hour. Besides, these reports were all the same. The son-of-a-bitch went out, lay around on his ass for a day or two, then snuffed some gooks from a few hundred yards away.

"Let's get on with it, Major. I'm sure Sergeant Rossen knows how to take care of leeches."

Hernandez barely concealed a thin grin at Tomlin's mention of leeches. "Very good, sir." He nodded at Rossen.

Taking a breath, he went on.

"At about 2200 of the third full night we had one or two VC come down the Hardball that we could positively identify as having weapons. By this time we had a pretty good-sized moon. About 2400 hours we got a lot of movement. There were some people coming down the Hardball and we saw some more up behind us on two sides through the nipa palms. They had apparently sent out flankers."

Hernandez saw Rossen's mouth twitch slightly at the corner, but he put it off as a nervous tic brought on by exhaustion.

For Rossen, it was a lot more. Knowing the enemy was in a position to cut you off from any support or get you in a crossfire was ass-hole puckering time. He knew he could depend on Tommy, but he had no way of telling for certain how the ST would react. They were supposed to be good, solid men, but this was an entirely different kind of pressure. By this time he knew everyone's nerves were stretched as thin as violin strings. He broke into a cold, clammy sweat as he moved ever so slowly to face to the rear. He could hear movement on two sides. There was no way for him to signal any orders to the ST. He could only hope they'd keep their cool and do as they'd been instructed and wait for him to start it, if there was to be any shooting.

He had two grenades with him, as did Tomanaga, one thermite for equipment destruction and a frag. Nodding to Tomanaga, he showed him his grenades and nodded. Tomanaga knew what he meant. They straightened out the cotter pins on their grenades and laid them where they'd be easy to reach. If the Dinks found them and there were too

many too handle, then they were to destroy
their sights, both the Adjustable Ranging
Telescope (the ART) and the Starlight.

He moved his body ever so slowly to the
right, where he could use the Starlight to
scope through a gap in his blind. The sounds
came closer. He thought to himself that mid-
night was as good a time to die as any
other. This was the bad part. Would they be
seen or just stumbled over? How many of
the Cong were out there? When should he
make the decision to open fire? On his side
of the blind he saw three men wearing the
standard-issue black pajamas and the faded,
floppy, greyish-green hats of the regular VC.
They had two AKs and an SKS assault rifle.
They walked within fifteen yards of Rossen
and his men. They played dead and he
prayed to God no one would cough or fart.
When they passed by and the sounds of
traffic on their other flank faded, it was
also difficult to control the nervous spasms
that set into arms and legs.

Rossen followed the flankers with his scope
as they moved down to the Hardball and
joined with the people there. He was able
to get a count for the first time. There were
twenty-three men on the Hardball; they
talked a couple of minutes, then moved on.
Again he had to resist the temptation to
bring them under fire. But he had seen this

several times before and knew they were exactly what he thought they were—a scouting party. Patience now! Don't blow your cool and you'll get what you've been waiting for.

Another hour passed during which he thought about whether he was ready to die or endure the worst of boogieman dreams. What if he was taken alive? Would he have the guts to surrender or would he kill himself? There were many things worse than death.

Shortly after 0100 hours they picked up a group of men, about nine or ten in a party. They were not the same as those who had passed earlier. They were moving together, one behind the other. The third man in line appeared to be dressed a bit differently. His outline and movements were those of an older man, and he carried no weapons that were visible. That decided it. Rossen wasn't going to wait around any longer. If they weren't the ones he was supposed to be waiting for, then it was their tough luck. He was not going to go through another day and night.

To Tommy he whispered, "You hold it down for me. My first target will be the old man who is dressed different. He is number three."

Now it was better! He settled down be-

hind his rifle, adjusting the butt to his
shoulder, letting his mind slide into his work,
to become one with the rifle. Breathing
steadied; pulse slowed. In the ghostly glow
of the Starlight, Rossen separated himself
from the thought that he was killing an old
man. The old Viet was just another target.

He took him out at about four-hundred-
and-fifty meters. When the shot was fired
and he went down, everyone else on the
Hardball went down too. Rossen couldn't
tell whether he'd actually hit him or if the
old man had just hit the deck when he heard
the sonic crack as the round went by. He
didn't fire again. Patience, control. . . .

A few minutes later they were up again;
they all crowded around the one in the different uniform, as if helping him. Rossen
figured that he had just winged the old man.
He took two more really quick shots and
knew he'd nailed his target. Even through
the haze of the Starlight he could see the
old man's head explode. They began to
panic. One man broke and went back down
the trail from the direction they had come;
the rest hit the ground again. Every now
and then he would catch one sticking his
head up. He'd wait until he had a good
sight, then let him bust one. Before the evening was over, he had taken all nine of
them. The only one who'd gotten away was

the one who had gone back down the trail: smart bastard. Rossen was sure that he had gone for help. About 0230 hours Tomanaga picked up two more. Rossen was off the scope at the time, resting his eyes. Tomanaga nudged him. He'd spotted them as they were trying to get equipment off the bodies of those he had already taken out. He took them with two easy shots in their backs and that was thirteen for the night.

Hernandez moved in his chair; the squeaking jerked Rossen back once more. "What happened then, Sergeant?"

Rossen cleared his throat. He wanted a drink of water and the leech bites were beginning to itch.

"Well, sir, that was the last contact for the night. We played dead and didn't move till the sun came up. Then I had Tommy call for the relief company to come in. When they did, we went onto the Hardball with them and gathered up their weapons and papers, then loaded up in the choppers and came back. All in all, we made a real clean haul of it."

CHAPTER TWO

The insertion was clean. They hit a cold LZ and were off and moving before the dust settled. Rossen was glad that he'd made a recon over the area three days ago. It helped now as he signaled his team to follow him. Noise security had to be absolute. This area was held by Charlie and he had fought several battalion-sized incursions by the Americans to a standstill. It was clear that GIs were not welcome on the river. This was Charlie's turf.

The four men of the security team were already regretting their hasty action in volunteering for the mission, but the promise of a week's R&R in Hong Kong was a powerful incentive. Rossen and Tomanaga, his partner, were not given that offer. Rossen didn't care, even though it had been seven months since he'd last taken one, and that was in Singapore.

Looking over the members of the security team, he looked at Tomanaga and shook his head. For his part, Rossen almost wished that he didn't need them. They weren't used to this kind of action, or non-action, where the best weapon you had was patience. From now until they either nailed the party of Communist cadremen coming in or were spotted and forced to bug out, there would be no smoking, no talking and very little movement. If you had to take a crap, you'd do it in your hole and cover it up.

They reached the edge of the gorge. On the opposite side of the river was a trail leading along a ridge. To the north, a water-fall fell a couple of hundred feet to the river-bed below. It was narrow, but the flow of water through it was rough enough to cre-ate white-water rapids that swirled around large grey boulders. That was good; the sound of the waterfall and rapids would help muffle any sounds of gunfire and maybe give them a little more time in the event of an enemy response to their ambush. If the Dinks came this way, they'd have to take the trail up to the top where they'd reach the plateau. He was sure they'd come this way. It was the easiest and best route from the junction with the Ho Chi Minh Trail where it split—one road heading farther to the south and the other coming into Vietnam from Laos. From what he had been told by G2, the cadremen had come a long way for this meeting. All the way from Peking. They would be impatient to reach their destination, and being this close in what Charlie considered to be a secure area, they would be tired and less alert. If they were all these things, then they'd take the easy way up the ridge, and when they did, he'd kill them.

Tommy stayed behind, bringing up drag; he kept the security team in the middle. Twice he had to warn one of the riflemen to shut up. After the second time he whispered to the infantryman's back that if he said one more unnecessary word, he'd shoot him in the legs and leave him behind when they pulled out. The others in the security team overheard him, and from that moment on there were no more problems with noise.

Rossen moved them alongside a native trail, trying to stay at least ten meters away from it. Trails were dangerous; too many things could happen on them. Only fools stayed to the trails in Charlie land. They didn't use machetes to cut through brush like they did in the movies. They didn't break branches as they passed, but used the terrain like a glove. They slipped and slid, ducked and twisted under, through, and around all barriers. Don't fight the jungle; use it. Leave as little sign as possible to show that anyone has ever passed this way.

The security team tried to emulate him and Tomanaga. Now that they were really in the field as backup for these crazy shits, it was suddenly terribly, terribly lonely. They realized quickly that the best chance they had to get back alive was to obey, without question or thought, the orders of the Sergeant and his partner. If they were told to squat, they'd squat.

It took them more than two hours to cover the five clicks from the LZ to where they got their first look at the river and the ridge on the opposite bank. Time for a breather. Rossen had the security team move to the rear and set up a watch. He and Tomanaga scoped the area around them, each taking a part of the visible terrain and sweeping it carefully. Nothing! The only things to be seen were shadows and one wild pig going to the edge of the river bank to drink. The pig was the best indicator that the area was clean and clear, at least for the time being. Leaving Tomanaga behind, he moved down the side of his ridge. Taking his time, he stopped every few minutes and made another sight sweep, and at each stop he looked back the way he had come to see what the enemy would see if they were there. Tomanaga kept him in his sights, following his movements as Rossen moved around the ridge checking for ways that Charlie could use to try to reach them if they were spotted from the other side.

Moving through spotty brush, he picked a spot just off the lip of the plateau and settled behind a cluster of jagged, waist-high boulders not yet worn smooth by time and weather. It was a good night for scoping. The moon was nearly full and the skies crystal clear. Through the Starlight scope, the natural green of the plant life looked eerie. Rocks, even the froth of the boiling waters below, were a ghostly shade of green in the scope.

Taking out a pad and pen, Rossen began to make a rough sketch of the area. The other side of the gorge was about three-hundred-and-twenty meters off in a straight line. He moved the Starlight down the trail, taking note of where it turned off. Anyone there would be out of sight. Then he traversed the scope back up the other end, to where the trail again turned into a crevice that led to the top. Anyone in there would also be safe. The killing zone had to be the stretch of about sixty feet between those two points. It wasn't perfect, but it was the best they had. There was some cover for their targets, a few boulders and a narrow ditch, formed by the rains that ran along the wall side of the trail, where they could take cover. He knew that his position for the ambush had to be at a higher elevation than the trail that the cadre and their escort would be on. That should give him an advantage, as far as being able to reduce the benefits they might have from the ditch and boulders on the south side of the ravine.

Sliding sideways along the ridge, he found a narrow animal track leading to the bottom. Carefully he memorized every spot from which the enemy might be able to come at them and then marked it on his hand-drawn chart. Then he clambered back up the trail, using vines and handholds to get up to Tomanaga.

Head to head, they talked softly about a site they both agreed on, one that gave them maximum natural cover. He would have liked to have had the protection that the boulders on their side of the gorge could have given them, but they were in the wrong place. They settled on a site where a couple of logs had fallen, a bit to the right of and above the trail leading down to the river.

Tomanaga went off to gather some brush and leaves to finish off what nature had started. As always, he went at least two hundred meters away from the site to gather the camouflage materials, and even then he would never take too much from any one spot. If Charlie were to notice that a large section of grass had been pulled out or cut or that a tree had been stripped of too many branches, it would have been a dead giveaway.

Rossen had Tomanaga take the security team and place the men in two different spots, one flanking their shooting site and the other a few meters to the rear. From there they'd be able to cover them if things got shitty, yet still be able to give hand signals to communicate with them during the daylight hours. Rossen didn't like using the HT1 radios any more than was absolutely necessary.

By dawn they had their positions camouflaged and Tomanaga helped the security team fix up their placements. He had to rearrange some of the branches so the bottom of the leaves stayed down. The security team people thought it was pretty nit-picking shit to get their asses chewed out over which way some damned leaves faced, but to Tomanaga—and men with trained eyes—the difference in color between the bottom of the leaves and the top of them was important enough to mean living or dying. It was the small things that killed you.

After he had them squared away, it was time to settle in. There was no way of knowing how long they might have to wait. Intell had not been very specific about the time or even the day when the big shots would be coming. It could be in the next hour, or a week from now. That was the max they would stay out. If the targets didn't show by then, they'd move out. Till then, all they could do was wait. . . .

During the next four days and nights, the members of the security team learned more about themselves than they would ever have believed possible to do in such a short time— time that seemed like weeks. They learned that they could take a crap and bury it like an animal. They learned to eat cold, tasteless food and to be thirsty, their lips drying and cracking, although they had full canteens at their sides. If they drank their fill during the day, then there would be no more, even though just below them was a river running full. They learned to spend hours lying in one spot with the sun pounding down on them. The corners of their eyes filled with the same fine grit that seeped into the seams of their uniforms and ground at every joint like sandpaper. Their eyes ached and fogged as they strained to see through a heat haze that rode in waves over the land. Two of them swore to give up smoking when they got back. They didn't want to have to go through withdrawal again.

The only time they were permitted to rise was at night; for a few minutes they moved to gather fresh cover for their camouflaged positions to replace the dried materials with new grass and leaves. Just to stand up was an almost indescribable luxury, though when they did, the muscles in their legs and thighs burned from the long daylight hours of being cramped up, unable to do much more than turn over. The only intercourse they had with Rossen and Tomanaga was the once daily, pre-dawn radio check they made with an L-19 that stayed just at the limit of the radio's reach. When they moved out, it would be the radio link with the small single-engined plane that would relay the order for the choppers to come in and get them at one or the other of their pick-up sites.

And they'd learned to hate the two men who had brought them to this. Each of them would more than likely have taken off if it hadn't been for the others. The fear of being a coward in the eyes of your friends was a powerful motivator, one that had over the ages made millions of frightened men into heroes in thousands of forgotten wars.

Then there came real fear. Fear that grasped at the gut with ice cold hands: the knowledge that if you were hurt or wounded you'd probably be left behind or, if you were lucky, be killed by your own men before they pulled out.

This time the fear came as they lowered their bodies deeper into their shallow pits, hoping that eyes couldn't see them through their cover of leaves and branches. They were thankful that they had done as they had been told and had gathered fresh cover every night. Eyes grew sweaty, as did armpits and hands. Fingers rested on safeties as each expected a cry of discovery every second.

Rossen and Tomanaga watched the VC patrol as it moved between them and their security team, hoping no one would get trigger-happy. Rossen saw one of the Viets move to the edge of the plateau and signal with a wave of his Kalashnikov to the opposite bank. He followed the Bo Doi's wave, seeing three men on the other side.

They moved on, and hearts slowed back to normal. Rossen felt it was a good sign. They had probably been making a sweep to make certain the area was clear for the cadremen. They had also been too fast and careless, confident that no Americans would be found in this, one of their strongholds, where they had always held their own. *That was good. Very good. If they were careless, then maybe the party he was waiting for would be also.*

The Viet sweeping patrol passed on out of sight. After a few minutes three men came back down the trail on the other side of the gorge, picking their way carefully to avoid the slick, damp rocks and tripping vines that tried to entangle their feet. Rossen knew instinctively that they were going back to lead the rest of a larger party up the trail. This was it! If it had been just a regular sweep they would have just gone on. Another hour passed. . . .

It was hard to control the trembling in his hand as he focused his binoculars on the figures approaching the killing zone. To Tomanaga he whispered, "They're coming. My God, there's at least three men in Red Chinese army uniforms with them in the center."

He did a count as they labored up the narrow trail. Fourteen of them, all well-armed. One carried a radio that looked a lot like an American PRC-10. They were moving slowly, breathing heavily from the exertion of the steep climb.

Not taking his eyes from them, he hissed at Tomanaga: "This is how it goes down. I want all of them, and the only way we can do it is to box up both ends so they can't move, then take out the center when we've got them pinned down. You take the one bringing up drag, and I'll take the point.

"Next I want that radio. Maybe I can take it and the operator out at the same time. From there work into the center."

He clicked the switch on his radio twice to let the security team members know they were getting ready to fire.

To the west, the setting sun had already begun to cast long shadows across the ravine. It would be dark in less than half an hour. He laid his sight on the first target, the point man leading the others up the trail. He'd take him out just before he reached the spot where the trail curved in and out of sight. Tomanaga would wait till he got off his first round before taking the tail. In the sight of the ART, the Charlie was clear. At this range Rossen could almost make out the pores in his skin. The point man was nearing the curve. Rossen took his breath, held it, then began to take in the slack.

His mind slipped into sync with his weapon. He wasn't truely conscious of the moment when the last of the trigger slack was gone. The recoil of the rifle was the first indicator that the shot was made. In the sight, which brought the Dink up close, he saw the round hit right at the junction of the lower right scapula. The Dink was lifted clear off his feet and flung sideways. A burst of red beat him to the gorge wall as his lungs were blown out of him. Rossen moved the sight to his right smoothly, unhurriedly. The Charlies had frozen. The radio man looked confused. Rossen's next shot took him right through the chest, exploding the radio as the round flattened out inside the man and exited through it. *Good! That should buy them some more time.*

The Charlies began to bump into each other as they tried to decide what to do. Tomanaga took out the tail man with a throat shot, nearly ripping the man's head off, and Rossen let the next in line take one in the chest. Across the gorge, the cadre and their escort were in the beginning of a state of panic, not knowing which way to go.

Two Charlies tried to return fire, but hadn't yet spotted Rossen and Tomanaga's position. Each of them went down with head shots. That did it. The Chinese took cover, exactly where Rossen thought they would, right behind the boulders. The rest of the escort took what cover they could and began to fire back across the ravine. They still didn't know where to shoot; they were just firing blind. Three rounds came over his head, he could hear the sonic crack as they passed.

Rossen took another one under fire. In

the scope, the man's face exploded as the 173 grain boattail round entered it right under his nose, traveling at a speed of 2550 feet per second.

A man tried to break and make it back down the trail. He didn't get more than ten feet before Tomanaga took him out. The Dink's body hit the gorge wall and bounced back to fall over the side of the cliff, smashing against the rocks in the riverbed below.

Rossen was pleased. The sound of the return fire was muffled by the vacuum-cleaner roar of the waterfall and river. The sounds of firing would not carry very far. The shadows grew longer, reaching across the ravine. Rossen knew the Charlies were probably counting on the coming darkness to be able to make a break for it. He laid down a few more rounds to keep them in place. Only one of them hit and killed; another blew off an exposed knee cap. Tomanaga shifted over to his Starlight scope. In a few minutes it would be dark enough for the light-gathering device to be used effectively.

The security team members were on edge. It was hard not being involved with the action. They had been briefed in detail and knew that their only job was to give cover and assist if needed . . . which would probably only happen if the VC had any patrols out in the area that could advance on their rear and get up up on the ridge with Rossen and Tomanaga. Then they'd all be in the shit. They had to stay where they were, though it was still rough on the nerves.

Rossen waited, giving them time to settle down. The Charlies were taking cover behind the boulders, not showing themselves. He knew that if he waited long enough, their nerves would force them into moving. Just be patient, he told himself. Don't think about a reaction force of VC coming to help them; don't think about the thousand unknown, unexpected things that could go wrong. Just concentrate on the targets and wait.... He had them where he wanted them. He knew that it might have been smarter to go ahead and just take out the three Chinese, but he wanted all of them, and he'd have them.

Tomanaga watched his partner for a second, then returned his eye to his scope, as Rossen also switched over from his ART to his Starlight. Tomanaga didn't know much, if anything, about the man he'd been with for the last six months. They didn't party together; they didn't go on R&R together; they didn't whore or drink or do anything together. Except kill. A couple of times he had tried to get closer to Rossen, but there was never any response. Not rejection, only a vacuum of feelings that left Tomanaga

knowing there was no place for him in
Rossen's life, except when they went into
the field. But maybe it was better that way.
He had the feeling that if he was permitted
to get closer to his partner, he might not
like what he found. Or, even worse, become
more like him. There was a coldness to
Rossen that made people stay away from
him. Tomanaga didn't understand just what
it was. There were others who had killed,
so what was the difference? Was it the
numbers Rossen had taken out? Or was
it that the rest were ordinary combat soldiers and Rossen was a killer and those he
served with felt that it really didn't make
any difference to him if it was a Charlie in
his scope or one of them? Tomanaga wasn't
certain about that either; but, if he had to
go in the field, then he would still rather
have Rossen as his partner than anyone else
in or out of the country. He was the best,
and he played the game better than anyone
else he knew. Perhaps that was it. The
game. . . .

Rossen did a count. They had nine down,
five to go, and one of those didn't have a
kneecap. He wondered what the men on the
other side of the gorge were thinking. If he
were the Chinese, he'd order at least one of
the two Viets able to walk to make a break
for it and try to bring back help. He wet his

lips with a sticky tongue. He wanted a drink of water, but this was not the time to take his eyes off the targets. A man could cover a lot of ground in just a few seconds. No, he'd wait and drink later. It shouldn't be long now.

The moon was full rise now. Through the Starlight, it was something like watching a world made up of phantoms, of the shining, green spirits of trees and leaves, of brush and rocks that still had traces of the day's heat seeping from them. Below him mist had begun to rise from the river, drifting slowly up to thin out and settle beads of moisture on his hands and face, but he waited. On the surface, his body was relaxed. A tense body took longer to respond. He forced his muscles to be at ease, thinking them into a relaxed, easy state that rested on the surface of his subconscious, so that he wouldn't have to think about what to do, for his body would know and it would do the right thing without the normal hesitation that premeditation inflicts on the nervous system.

The Viets broke. The two able-bodied men had both taken off at the same time, one going up the trail, one down. Rossen's finger moved before his mind had fully registered Charlie's actions, but he didn't bother to follow the shot with his scope. He knew when it was right. It just felt good.

Not thinking, he let his "other self" take over. Smoothly, almost slowly, the scope moved to the left. Again the finger squeezed of its own volition, taking up the slack in the trigger as the scope traversed. The recoil of the M-14 thumped against his shoulder. This time he held the sight on the target. The man was hit. The round had taken him on the left hip, blasting out a gobbet of meat and bone. The Viet screamed, but the sound didn't travel across the ravine. In the green haze of the scope, Rossen could see his target's open mouth twisted in agony as he fell back against the side of the mountain. The mouth was a darker green shadow than the flesh around it. The finger moved again and a round entered the darkened cavity, exploding the man's head. To Rossen, it looked like what happened when one held a ripe grape between the fingers and popped it.

Tomanaga hadn't fired. He had blinked at the time the Viets had moved. He heard Rossen's first shot, and by the time he focused his eyes again, the second round had gone off; then came the third. By then he was also on the target and he saw Rossen's round hit the Viet in his open mouth and knew that the last shot had gone exactly where Rossen wanted it. It all went down in a distorted time that seemed like a full minute at least, but had, in real time, taken less than four seconds.

Not taking his eye from his scope, he grunted. "Rossen, how you gonna get those chinks? It don't look like they're going to show enough to get a shot at. And I don't like hanging around here. We've been lucky so far, but sooner or later them gentlemen are going to be missed, and when they are, we better not be here."

Rossen wondered for a moment: *Why does Tomanaga always called Chinese "chinks"? But then, the Orientals were supposed to be an inscrutable race.*

He took his rifle from his shoulder and rubbed his eyes. "Simple enough, Tommy. I'm going to go and get them. You just pop a cap every now and then to keep them in place and I'll be right back. Then we can get the fuck out of here."

Tomanaga didn't like it, but Rossen was the team leader, and if he wanted to climb down the damned mountain and go up the other side and personally kill four men, then who was he to argue with him? And they said Orientals were hard to understand!

"Just make it fast, partner!"

Rossen didn't answer. He was already sliding over the side and heading for the bottom.

Tomanaga didn't watch him. He kept his attention on the cluster of boulders where the three Chinese and the wounded Viet lay hiding. He was getting a bit more concerned about Rossen. He was breaking some of the rules of the game by exposing himself and going after the Chinese. That wasn't good. He'd have to decide what to say in his after-action report. Maybe Rossen was going over the edge and needed to be sent Stateside before he got himself, or even worse, his partner, killed.

Taking care to protect his rifle, Rossen slid and slipped down the narrow trail. It took nearly fifteen minutes to reach the bottom. Twice he heard shots above him that meant Tomanaga was on the job. Near the river he took another scope of the area. Seeing nothing to stop him, he crossed. The current was swift, but the water wasn't very deep, not rising much over his thighs. He still had to fight the current, using the back side of the froth-swept boulders to break the worst of the current. Placing one foot after the other, he carefully felt the bottom before making each move. He was soaked, not just with the river spray, but with the sweat his body heat had created on the climb down. The river helped to cool him off. It was a temptation to lower his body all the way in. Keeping his rifle above his head, he waded on across to the other side.

Once there, he kneeled for a moment, taking cover behind a cluster of rocks and brush. Taking a long, slow breath to let his breathing slow back to normal, he waited for the pounding in his chest to level off to a dull throb. Gulping down several more deep breaths of air to catch his second wind, he began to climb. Staying off the VC's trail, he clambered up the side of the cliff, his rifle slung crossways over his shoulder. Using handholds and vines to help support his weight, he searched for footholds in the dark and found them. Arms and legs vibrating with the strain, he came back on the Viet trail, ten meters from the spot where it made the bend that led to the killing zone.

He felt hot; his face was flushed from the climb up. There had been no response from the Chinese. He figured that any sounds of his climb had been covered by the river and waterfall.

Placing his back against the cliff wall, he unslung his rifle, took the safety off, and began to inch his way around the curve.

Tomanaga scanned the trail and saw Rossen begin to make his move. He didn't have to be told what to do. Putting in a fresh magazine, he opened fire, sending one round after another at the cluster of boulders. Sparks from ricochets flickered as bullets sang off the rocks to fly into the night or bury themselves in the side of the cliff. The muzzle flash from his rapid fire caused the automatic protective lens cover to click shut on the Starlight. It didn't matter—he wasn't going for accuracy.

Rossen knew that Tomanaga was emptying his magazine and was placing his shots at regular intervals of one second each to give him time to count. When the last round was shot off, he stepped around the curve and moved at a half-crouch, his rifle at hip level. He was on the Chinese while they still had their heads lowered far below the level of the protecting boulders. They were close together, huddled on their knees. Each had a weapon, but they never had time to use them. Rossen opened up, letting each of them hold two rounds. One in the chest, another in the head. It was almost too easy. . . .

Only one still moved, the Viet with the torn-off kneecap. Dragging his bad leg, he tried to get away from the death that was coming. His back hitting the wall of the gorge stopped him. All he could see in the dark was a huge black shadow standing in front of him. He covered his eyes with both hands, afraid to look.

Rossen didn't bother to raise the rifle to

his shoulder. Lungs sucking air, face and back running with sour sweat, he took his time. Keeping the weapon at hip level, he lowered the bore just a fraction and ever so slowly squeezed off one round. The bullet smashed through the whimpering Viet's hands, taking him right at the bridge of the nose. His head snapped back; the hands dropped. Rossen stood over him as the legs trembled in the death spasm and the bowels and bladder let loose, soiling the man even further in death.

Ignoring the foul odor, Rossen searched the bodies of the Chinese, removing all documents and papers from them and putting them all into a brown leather musette bag one of them had carried. He ripped the insignia off the jacket of one of them and stuffed it into his pocket. He wanted proof that his kills were Chinese and not Vietnamese. Maybe the papers would prove it, and maybe not, but the rank badges with their insignia were proof positive.

Tomanaga witnessed the last kill through his scope. He felt a chill as he watched Rossen execute the last man. He knew it was necessary, but still, it was so cold. It was different from taking them at a distance, even though you could see your kill in the scope. But just standing right there made it very personal and private, almost a sexual thing . . . almost a sexual thing. . . .

CHAPTER THREE

Rossen made the return trip. As he neared, Tomanaga broke radio silence to the security team.

"Get ready to move out."

It was with relief that Johnston answered back. "Shit, man, I was ready to leave three days ago, but now it looks like we have even more of a reason to do it. I hear movement to your right flank. Company is coming."

Tomanaga grabbed up their gear and hissed to Rossen. "Hurry it up, they're coming."

Rossen knew that Tommy wasn't talking about the Red Cross. Lunging up over the top, he took Tomanaga's hand. Not looking back, they took off, picking up the security team on the way. They had miles to go before they reached their initial pickup site. There was no help to be had along the way. The nearest friendly installation was a Special Forces "A" Team which had a camp thirty miles away.

They could hear voices behind them as commands were given. The Viet Cong weren't concerned about noise security. That meant there were enough of them that they didn't feel they had to take any special precautions. The VC wanted the snipers and wanted them bad. Someone's ass was going to be on the line for letting the Chinese get snuffed. They had gone about two clicks before they finally broke free of the heaviest undergrowth, brush and trees. Now they were on a rolling plain dotted with dark patches of trees and bamboo.

This was the dangerous part. They'd be in the open, and if Charlie had his shit together and a good radio network, it wouldn't take them long to locate the six Americans.

They ran, hearts pounding. Their only real chance was to move fast enough to get far enough ahead of the pursuers to have a shot at making their radio contact with the relay plane in the morning. Rossen checked his watch. There were still too many hours till dawn and the brightness of the moon was now against them. Visibility in the clear would be well over two hundred meters.

In the dark, sound is deceptive. He heard a cry of discovery. The voice could have been a hundred meters behind them or five hundred. Scattered shots cracked flatly to their rear and right flank, sounding more like a kid's firecrackers than anything else. Charlie was trying to spook them, to flush them out of the brush.

Another mile and they had to stop. Forming a small perimeter, the security team spread out. Johnston lay on his stomach. Bile rising up to the back of his mouth made him swallow several times quickly to keep from upchucking. The last few days had done nothing for their wind or their legs.

"Well!" Johnston demanded angrily. "What now? How do we get out of here?"

Rossen took a small pull from his canteen. "We run if we can, fight if we have to."

Tomanaga knew what their options were. If they could stay in front of Charlie, they might be able to stretch them out. The weaker ones would not be able to keep up with the stronger and would fall behind. Then Rossen would turn on them. He'd seen it happen before. He'd be given charge of the security team to get them out and Rossen would stay behind to play. There was no arguing with the man. When you tried, he just looked through you as if you weren't really there and went on and did things his way anyhow.

They picked up the pace; there were still at least two hours before they'd be able to make contact with the relay plane and another one before a chopper could come in to get them.

They'd just hit the far edge of the field and were entering a patch of trees when a five-round burst went over their heads.

Rossen dropped to his knee in a clump of elephant grass to break up his outline. "Tomanaga, you go on ahead and take them to the alternate site. I'll hang back to slow the Dinks up a bit."

Tomanaga didn't bother to answer. He knew better. Pushing past the security team leader, he took point and plunged on ahead. The first pickup site was only ten or fifteen minutes' march, but it was still too long before an exfiltration could be made. They'd have to make it another six clicks to the next one.

Scoping across the field, Rossen clearly made out three shapes coming into the high grass. He drew down on the tail man, remembering the old Gary Cooper movie about Sergeant Alvin York, where he'd always shoot the rear turkey so as not to spook the one in front. That way York got all the birds or, in the movie, the Germans.

The rifle was shoved back deep against his shoulder. The suppressor reduced the crack of the rifle to where it didn't spook the oncoming VC. The rear man fell, his throat blasted open and the vertebrae connecting the head to the shoulder completely gone, leaving his head half-hanging on to his spine by a bloody ribbon of flesh. He was already sighting on the next man in line when the Dink stopped at the sound of his comrade collapsing. He stood wondering if his friend had slipped or stumbled into a hole. His brains erupted out of his forehead.

Rossen was traversing over to the lead man, taking up the pressure on the trigger, when the Dink hit the dirt. He'd seen the muzzle flash of Rossen's last shot.

Rossen scanned carefully, but couldn't bring him into the sight.

"Help! The sniper is over here. Come to me. Hurry!"

He didn't know what the words were but he damn sure knew what the VC was calling for.

Other voices answered the VC's cry for help and they weren't too far away. Time to move out. In a half-crouch, he followed after Tomanaga and the security team. Once inside the protective cover of the trees, he took time to bend over for a minute, take a grenade from his pouch and string it between a couple of trees.

Tomanaga kept pushing at the security team to keep them moving. Hearts straining, lungs aching, he forced them to take each step until Johnston could go no farther and just stopped in his tracks and sat down. The back of his tunic was stained with dark streaks of sweat. His face was pale under the glow of the bright moon.

"I'm not going another damned step. I've got to rest for a minute."

Tomanaga wasn't about to waste time arguing with the man. He jerked the M16 rifle from Johnston's slack hand and motioned to the others to follow him as he took the lead again.

Looking back over his shoulder at the sitting man, he hissed. "Stay as long as you like, but you're not getting your rifle back. No sense making a gift to Charlie of any more weapons."

He moved out. The other members of the team looked at each other with guilty, frightened eyes, then at the sitting man, and then followed after Tomanaga, knowing that at this time he was their only hope to get out of the jungle alive. The security team leader didn't take long to make up his mind before he was on feet and asking for his weapon back.

Rossen paused to change magazines. Before he had the fresh one in, a distant, dull thump, followed by a shrill, womanish cry, told him someone had hit the trip wire on his grenade and had been tapped. *Good! That should make them move a bit slower for a minute or two.*

He set out another grenade. This time he placed it under his pack. There wasn't anything in it that he'd need anymore—just a few rations and a change of socks. After scooping out a small, shallow grave in the dirt, he pulled the pin and set the grenade in the hole, placing it carefully under the pack so its weight would keep the lever down on the small bomb till someone picked up the sack.

It was wasted effort—he heard no other explosions and figured that the pursuers must have been a bit gun-shy of any offerings he'd made. He'd have to do something else. Increasing his speed, he wove and twisted his way along a narrow animal trail. Under normal circumstances he would never have stayed on any kind of a path, but the greatest danger, percentage-wise, was with the men coming behind him.

Resting his head against the weathered, rough trunk of a tall mango tree, its ancient body laced around with vines the thickness of a man's forearm, he tried to catch his breath and settle the throbbing in his chest where his lungs were trying to rip themselves out of the confining bones of his ribcage. Wiping the sweat from his face and eyes, he looked around. Glancing through the branches, he determined dawn was still a half-hour away and now the night was at its heaviest. The moon had set and the grey closeness of the pre-dawn was oppressive, thick, in his nose and mouth. He could taste the rich, sour-sweet ripeness of Asia in his pores.

He knew that Charlie was close on his ass. They'd be here in less than ten minutes. He needed to do something to break them up. He looked back up the trunk of the tree. A thin smile danced across his lips. He took the Chinese officer's leather musette case from his shoulders.

Placing his rifle against the tree, he forced shaking legs to push his body up to where he could pin the case on the end of a broken branch ten feet above the earth where it could be easily seen.

Knowing the enemy would be looking to

their front for him, he made a wide half-circle to his right and settled into a clump of yellow, waist-high grass on a low knoll. There was enough light now to switch over to the ART. Practiced hands twisted the knobs that released the Starlight scope and put it back into its case, and then replaced it with the ART. Putting it to his eye, he adjusted the sight, placing the reticule on the trunk of a tree. It was three-hundred-and-seventy meters from the knoll to the tree as determined by his rangefinder. Using some of the grass to stick in tufts around his body and legs for a bit of additional camouflage, he waited. It wouldn't be long before the VC reached the tree.

The lead Dink stepped warily out into the clearing. His body half-crouched over, he kept moving, bent to present as small a target as possible. One step, then another. At last, he straightened up and ran forward, zigzagging, till he reached the tree. Slamming his body up against the trunk, he looked out around it to the front, unaware that Rossen already had his spine in his sights.

Above Charlie's head the musette bag dangled from its shoulder strap. Seeing it, the scout waved back across the clearing and two more men ran to join him; then another two broke to each flank, this time not stopping at the tree. They ran on until they were in the trees at the far end. Then, and only then, did the ones Rossen wanted come forth with the main body of ten men. Moving much as the scout did, they reached the tree and stood under it, looking up at the leather bag. Caution was written in all their actions as they gestured and argued over what to do. The booby traps Rossen had set on his trail had made them justifiably wary.

Lying prone, he adjusted the tension on the rifle sling to where it gave the most support to his rifle. The VC around the tree were all dressed much the same. He couldn't make out any insignia of rank or anything equipment-wise to tell him who the brass was. That was the job the leather bag should do for him.

At last they came to a decision. The main body moved away from the tree to a safe distance as the man they'd selected shinnied up to the limb and very carefully looked over the bag and branch checking for any wires or booby traps. Seeing none, he slid the bag off very slowly with constant urging and advice from the spectators.

From across the clearing, the VC who had gone on ahead yelled back that the way was clear.

The Charlie with the bag slid carefully back down the trunk of the tree and walked on eggs over to the main body of men and set the bag on the ground. There was more gesturing and argument before one man finally got up enough nerve to take the bag, hold it to his head and shake it slightly and listen. He tried to feel through the leather, as if his fingers would be able to tell him the contents. They didn't. There was some advice passed on to him from the others, and he set the bag back down on the ground, took out a hunting-style knife from a leg sheath and slit the bottom of the bag open. Gingerly he felt around inside the bag with the fingertips of his right hand.

"There are only papers inside it, Comrade."

At that, two men came forward and took the bag from him. The contents were handed over to a middle-aged Charlie with an upper plate made from stainless steel. He took the map out of the case and opened it up.

Rossen let him hold one in the chest and swung his rifle back and forth as fast as he could pull the trigger. Three others went down—Rossen was firing so quickly that he didn't have time to really focus on his targets. He knew, though, that if they were hit, it was probably in the trunk of the body. There wasn't time for anything fancy. The suppressor had, as usual, worked well and the Viets weren't certain of where the shots had come from. Most of them still looked to the front, where their own men began to fan out and search the fringe of the trees and brush.

Rossen moved slowly, backing away down the obverse side of his knoll.

Using the small knoll for cover, he bent over and ran into the trees. Once there, he took his last grenade and tossed it as far as he could to his left. Not waiting for the explosion, he took off. Keeping to the trees, he moved out and away on an oblique course that he hoped would put him back on the trail that Tomanaga and the security team had taken to the alternate LZ.

The grenade exploding behind them brought the VC into action. They opened fire at the cloud of dust and grass the exploding grenade had thrown up. From across the field the Charlies came racing back, weapons at the hip, ready to fire, as they raced to give their ambushed comrades support.

Rossen could hear the Dinks cursing and shouting as he settled into a mile-eating lope. He had to put some distance between them or they'd catch up to him and the others as the chopper came in. If that happened, it would be unlikely that any of them would get out alive.

*   *   *

Tommy halted for a breather and to set up the radio. It was time for the relay plane to make its pass. Adjusting the squelch to reduce the static, he began to call.

"Boomer, Boomer. This is Alley Cat, do you read me? Over!"

Nothing.

He tried again, then cocked his head to see if he could pick up any engine sounds.

Nothing.

Checking his watch, he knew they had to be close. Risking it, he waited another five minutes and was just pressing the talk switch on the mike when he felt, more than heard, a thin, distant drone.

"BOOMER, BOOMER. This is Alley Cat. Do you read me? Over."

This time there came a crackling response from the L19 pilot.

"That's a Roger, Alley Cat. What's your status?"

"We did the job, now it's time for Papa Bear to come and get us at Alpha Two, and he'd better bring a couple of friends. We have company coming. Do you Roger that? Over."

"That's a big Ten Four, good buddy. Papa Bear is on the way with friends. Should I stay around for a while?"

"Negative. You might draw them to us. Just have Papa Bear there ASAP."

"Wilco, Alley Cat. Papa Bear should be on station in one hour. Luck to you guys. Out."

The L19 banked to the starboard and moved off. The pilot never saw the men on the ground, but he didn't envy them. An hour was a terribly long time when your ass was being chased by people who would dearly love to cut your balls off and stuff them in your mouth.

"Okay, you people, saddle up. If we keep moving, we'll be barely on time, and the taxis here don't keep their meters running." Tomanaga pushed the security team to its feet. Somewhere they found enough additional energy. Perhaps it was because they now believed they had a good chance to get out alive.

Checking his compass, Rossen picked out a landmark in the distance. Now that it was full daylight, visibility was what weathermen would call unlimited. He could see a single, green, round hill rising by itself to the southeast about ten clicks off. He had his bearings and moved out again. Head bent over, his mouth open, he tried to concentrate on his breathing, to inhale as much as possible through the nose. One step after the other was the only way to get there. His mind focused on that one thing. One step, then another. He ran, never changing his pace. The weight of his gear tried to drag him off to one side and then the other, but he wouldn't let it. *What was that?* A shadow passed over the grass in front of him.

He tried to look up, but with the salty sweat stinging in his eyes he couldn't see properly; everything was a foggy haze. He jerked his mind back to where it belonged. This was no good; he needed his eyes more than anything else. Wiping them clear with the sleeve of his jacket, he looked back up. Only then did the drone of the small engine break through the thick cloud that had been over his mind as he ran.

He knew Tomanaga must have made contact. That meant that he'd probably have about an hour to reach the LZ. If he wasn't there, it wasn't likely that the chopper would hang around very long waiting for him. Shaking his head to clear it, he listened. Hearing nothing, he forced his legs back into their pattern of one step after the other. This time it was harder to get started again. The brief pause had let the muscles in his thighs and calves grow leaden and dead. Pumping oxygen into his lungs, he went on. One more hour and he would be home free.

CHAPTER FOUR

Major Duyen Xien Ma was not pleased with the course of events. They should have had the Americans in their hands by now, and he had lost his second-in-command and two sergeants at the mango tree. There had been nothing of value in the case. The documents being brought in by the Chinese had been replaced by twigs and leaves. The *Phü Nhäm*, killer, still had the briefcase papers in his possession. If he failed to return with them, it could mean his own life. The loss of the Chinese advisors was bad enough, but the contents of those papers could set back their efforts to liberate the country by months—if not years. They were the plans and timetables for a general uprising to take place throughout South Vietnam. If they were not recovered, all of that would change and the uprising could not take place as planned.

From every detachment in the vicinity that had a radio he had men converging. He knew that the only way out for the Americans was by air, and that reduced their operations. There were only a few places where a helicopter could get in. One of them was already held by his men, and the other two were in front of him. The only question was which one were the *Ngui My* heading for. In addition to his other problems, the men with him were something less than eager to continue their tiger hunt. Too many of them had seen the effectiveness of the sniper's shooting. It was only with curses and threats of death or worse that he could whip his men on. The Tokarev pistol in his hand added emphasis to his demands for them to increase their speed. This was not a time for caution if they were to catch up.

He left the dead and wounded where they were. He needed all of his men for the pursuit. As the Indians did when they hunted a tiger, his men spread out like beaters, moving at a half-run where the terrain permitted. He didn't care if a few more of them got killed; the sound of gunfire would aid in guiding the rest to their quarry.

*   *   *

Tomanaga was on site. The LZ was a small, flat-topped rise that sat a few feet above the field of ten-foot-high elephant grass they had just come through. The ST took up positions in a tiny perimeter around the edge of it. Lying on their stomachs, they watched the grass for any movement. No one could get to them in the daylight without being noticed. The movement of the grass would give them away. Tomanaga stood up and looked back the way they had come and wondered how Rossen had made out. He'd heard the flat crack of Kalashnikov rifles when Rossen had made his hit at the mango tree and knew that his partner wouldn't hang around there very long. If he wasn't cut off or already dead, he'd be coming soon. He'd have to come soon; there were less than ten minutes left till the chopper was due. . . .

Rossen hit the high grass. He couldn't see the rise, but he knew it was just about two hundred meters ahead. He went in; the grass closed around him. Its thick, rough edges rasped like a cat's dry tongue against his face and hands. The tips of the grass moved gently as an easy morning breeze blew down from the north. His face was covered with a grey dust, through which streaking channels had been cut by the tiny rivers of sweat that ran off his face and forehead.

Johnston felt like shit; every bone in his body ached. He was tired, thirsty, hungry, scared. His fingers were slippery as he held on to the trigger of his rifle. He stared at the wall of grass, as if expecting a division of Cong to come charging out of it at any moment. The rest of the ST were in no better shape. Every movement of the wind through the tops of the grass brought a momentary spasm of terror.

Tomanaga was manning the radio, his eyes scanning the horizon for any sight of the rescue choppers.

Johnston's eyes clicked to the left across the field. The grass moved, but this time it was a different movement than that of the wind. His eyes fogged over; his body tensed. He wasn't even aware that his finger was tightening on the trigger of his M16 until the rifle stammered back against his shoulder. He put a full magazine out in the direction of the movement. When he opened fire, so did the rest of the ST. They didn't know what they were shooting at, but somehow just firing made them feel better, to be doing something at last.

Tomanaga ran over to Johnston, who was frantically trying to reload with fingers that were suddenly much too large and numb for him to have any coordination in an act he'd done a thousand times in practice. Tommy kicked him in the side of the head with his boot, knocking him over to his back, and placed his rifle bore right on Johnston's sweating forehead.

"You dumb shit. Who told you to fire?"

The rest of the team had quit firing at Tomanaga's movement.

Johnston tried to point over his shoulder at the grass.

"I saw them coming. The grass, it was moving. . . ."

Tomanaga looked to where Johnston had been pointing. He didn't see anything. But then a muffled, angry voice yelled at him. "Hey, you dumb sons-a-bitches, what the fuck do you think you're doing?"

It was Rossen! Tomanaga yelled for him to come on in. There was little need for silence now. Every Dink in five miles knew they were there.

Duyen Xien Ma halted in his tracks, turned to face slightly northeast and pointed with his pistol.

"They are there!"

The distinctive flat rapid chatter of M16s on full auto removed any doubt in his mind that his own troops had fired with AKs or SKS assault rifles. To his radio operator he gave the order to tell all of his search parties to converge on the sound of the M16s. He was very close now. With the blessings of the *Than Tien* and his ancestors, he would have them before the next hour had passed.

Rossen joined Tomanaga on the knoll. "What's the score? Did you make contact with the relay?"

Tomanaga nodded. "They're on the way, should be here in less than ten minutes."

"They better be, because every goddamned Dink in twenty miles in gonna be on our ass."

He would have chewed them out more, but figured that one or more of them stood a good chance of dying in the next few minutes for their mistake. That was a high enough price and one that they'd remember in the future . . . if there was going to be a future for them.

Major Duyen pushed his men, lashing them with his tongue, alternately praising and cursing them. Two other parties were converging on a large field of elephant grass. That would have to be the pickup site; there was no other place within easy range that helicopters could get in and out of. All other sites close enough had already been prepared for such an incursion, with sharpened stakes hidden in the high grass to prevent any aircraft from touching down. The stakes would impale it like a sacrificial animal. It had to be the field known as Lam Thung. There he would find them, if he moved fast enough. He didn't know why they had fired and didn't care. Perhaps one or more of his scouts had stumbled on them. It didn't matter.

"*Di, Di!* Go, go!" He whipped his men forward. His RTO kept in constant communication with the other two units. Between them they would have sixty-three men. Major Duyen was satisfied. Even with expert shots such as the *Phü Nhām*, he would have them. Fire power was on his side. Each of the groups had one light machine gun and one sixty mm mortar with them. They would be able to keep the Americans pinned down and pound them into jelly from a safe distance. If necessary, however, he was willing to spend every life in his command in a mass attack. He would throw men at them so fast they wouldn't have time to reload.

Whatever the cost in lives, he would have the papers the Americans had stolen from the bodies of the dead Chinese advisors.

Rossen never took his eyes from his scope. He knew they were close. The throb of the approaching choppers grew stronger. Tomanaga yelled at him.

"Hey, Rossen, we got some muscle. The Slick's got three Cobras riding shotgun with him."

Rossen's rifle bucked. "We're going to need them. Guess who's coming to dinner and wants to eat our ass up."

Major Duyen was knocked over backwards. Rossen's shot had taken the man in front of him dead in the chest. If it hadn't been for the canteen strapped to the back of the man's pack, the round would have gone clean through and hit him. He scurried on all fours till he could take cover behind a tree. Where had the shot come from? To the north he heard some firing. His RT man told him it was the rest of the searchers converging on the field. They had seen the Americans on a rise directly in front of Duyen's position. Duyen listened to the sky and knew that he would have to hurry.

He cried out to all within earshot and his

radio man relayed his words to the other units.

"Into the grass. It is high enough to give us cover from the snipers. Those with mortars set up and give us covering fire on the mound. When the helicopters come over, aim for the pilots' compartments. Now move!"

Mortar rounds began to arch slow and lazy overhead, landing with flat thumps some distance behind the mound as the Viet mortar crews ranged their target. The enemy's fire from their light weapons was less of a bother. The Charlies in the grass couldn't see shit. They were just firing wild. From their vantage point, Tomanaga and Rossen had a much better view and took full advantage of it. They switched their magazines, slapping in ones filled with tracers. Johnston and the rest of his team set up around the mound with instructions to watch where Rossen and Tomanaga shot —then they were to lay fire on the same place.

The mortar rounds were being walked in. Hot shrapnel sang overhead as the explosions came closer.

Rossen yelled to Tomanaga, "Get back on the horn and tell those Cobras to take out the mortars or there won't be enough of us left here to fill one body bag."

The unarmed Slick lay back as the Cobras moved on target in response to Tomanaga's call for help. They followed the bright, streaking tracks of his tracers to the edge of the woods where the Viet mortar crews had set up their sixties.

The Cobras followed the streaks of Tomanaga's tracers and laid down a withering barrage from their mini-guns. The Viet mortar crews were ripped apart as thousands of rounds a minute poured from miniguns' barrels.

The flight leader snapped over his mike to the others in his flight. "Hey, boys, let's have a barbecue. Make like an Indian and start circling them. I want this whole field to burn, baby. Burn!"

The Cobras came in overhead at less than a hundred feet, mini-guns roaring. Burning tracers guiding their shots, they swept across the field like scythes. Rockets from pods puffed grey smoke briefly to the rear, then streaked out to explode in clusters of brilliant red fire among Duyen's men. The grass began to burn behind them. Two of the gunboats banked into a sharp orbit and came in on a line in front of the snipers and their back-up team. Tracers created hundreds of tiny fires in the dry elephant grass. Flames began to grow, shooting up the dry, ten-foot-tall stems to lick at the sky. The slight wind fed the flames and they began to spread rapidly in a burning wall.

Rossen ordered his men to throw their grenades. He and Tomanaga had the only white phosporus grenades. These they tossed to either side of their mound to help the flames get a good hold. When all grenades had been expended, they went back to rifle fire. Rossen directed their shots into the grass.

"Keep it low, you dumb shits!"

Around the the Cong the choppers circled like hungry vultures who had grown tired of waiting. The pilots and their crews were jubilant. It wasn't often they had a chance like this, where the Dinks were in the open. They circled the field, setting it on fire in all directions, forcing the Viets into a single, ever-constricting circle. The choppers dove and swept over them, the mini-guns ripping bodies into shreds that lay and quivered in the smoking grass till the flames reached them and added the juice of their bodies to the dry clouds of smoke rising into the once clear skies.

The Viets were burning. . . . Several tried to break though the wall of flames surrounding them. They had long since dropped their weapons. Clothes and hair on fire, they stumbled blind across patches of earth now charred black and smoking where the flames had eaten away the elephant grass. Tomanaga and Rossen took them under fire with well-placed single shots.

Johnston stood on his feet crying at the choppers. "Give it to them! Burn the little bastards. Burn them!" His mouth was still open, screaming, when his body erupted. It simply exploded. From his waist to his neck, he was ripped apart, blood spraying into the air, a red mist.

The chopper pilot cursed his aim. Smoke had hampered his vision for a moment and he'd put out one short burst from the mini-gun that had gone a bit high.

From the north, the wind strengthened. The flames turned into a cyclone of searing heat that sucked the air from the lungs of the encircled Viets. From their place on the rise, it felt to Tomanaga, Rossen and their men as though they were facing into a blast furnace.

Duyen whirled around in a circle of pain. His uniform was charring on his back, burning into the flesh of his skin. His rubber-soled boots had melted to the bottoms of his feet. The pain was beyond anything he had ever known could exist. The bullets in his pistol exploded in their magazine, blasting the pistol apart, sending pieces of metal into his thigh. He never felt them. The nerve endings were already dead and charred, as were the muscles in his calves and thighs, now shriveled and shrunken under the heat, forcing him onto his knees, hands raised in front of eyes that could no longer see them. They had turned to black clawed talons.

The ocean of fire washed over him and his surviving men in waves, halted a moment to feed on their flesh, then moved on till the walls of flame met each other and merged into one last great swirling tornado that sucked dust and ash high into the clear sky. The flames fed on each other until there was no more to feed them, and they too died.

The Slick came in, barely touching down. Rossen found Johnston's dogtags and pulled them off of his neck. He thought a moment about taking the body back with them, shrugged his shoulders, and climbed on board with the others. Let Graves Registration worry about retrieving the cadaver. He was through for the day.

Around them the gunboats still hovered, like angry wasps wanting more targets. Over their intercoms the crews congratulated each other and promised to buy drinks for the entire base when they got back.

Weary, ST members leaned back against the canvas seats, their heads resting against the faded red padding. Faces black with streaks of soot and ash, they each emptied what remained in their canteens. Tomanaga looked over at Rossen and winked, then said with great sincerity to the surviving men: "Hey, you guys, you done pretty good out there. Want to go out with us again in a couple of days?"

Even Rossen found a thin smile at the sudden burst of swearing that came from the terrified troops. He and Tomanaga would never see them again.

Behind them, the fires had nearly burned out. The Viets were clustered together in heaps, their bodies smoking, limbs twisted and contorted, lips drawn back from teeth or burned away to leave the dead with obscene smiles on their faces. The smoke drifted away from the clearing to where the family of pigs, which had hidden in a thicket when the shooting started, lay waiting. To them, the smell of burned bodies meant food. It would be some time yet before they gathered enough courage to venture out. But soon they would and then they would feed on the cooked flesh the Cobras had left for them.

CHAPTER FIVE

Lieutenant Colonel Tomlin admired his handiwork. He had already used it for the briefing of two congressmen this morning. It proved beyond the shadow of a doubt the value of the sniper program and how cost-effective it was. Now it was almost time to welcome back Sergeants Rossen and To-managa. He didn't really care for Rossen very much, but, then, no one else he knew did either. As for Tomanaga, he was much better to deal with. But, after all, Orientals were taught as children to be respectful of their superiors. Still, Rossen was quite valu-able to his program, and if he did things in an unorthodox manner, it didn't matter very much, not as long as his kill ratio was maintained.

Standing back away from his desk, he reexamined the easel with the large cardboard chart on it. The chart listed quite clearly the number of kills for each sniper under his command. Topping the list was Rossen, who, for some reason after he had taken his last out-of-country R&R, had really settled into his work, with sixty–four confirmed, and probably a dozen more that weren't. A shuffling behind him broke his stream of thought. Irritated, he barked at the sixty-one-year-old Annamite cleaning woman emptying the ashtrays filled with cigar ash from the morning's briefing. "Get out. You can do that after I go to lunch."

Obediently, with her back perpetually bent from a lifetime of bending over, the black pajama-clad woman bowed her way out of the presence of the light Colonel as she had done nearly every day since she had come to work for the Americans two years before. She was almost a piece of furniture, something no one noticed or paid any attention to, except when they needed something cleaned up or a quick spit shine put on their boots.

Once she was gone, Lieutenant Colonel Andrew Tomlin again reviewed his new chart with pleasure. Charts were good. With charts the world could be made to run more smoothly. Major problems could be explained away with columns of neat figures, graphs and statistics. Casualties could be put into their proper perspective, showing that their losses weren't really that bad.

Yes! Charts certainly were a marvelous device: clean, neat, almost pristine.

His intercom buzzed to notify him that Rossen and Tomanaga were in the outer office waiting to report.

"Send them in." It was strange how good it made him feel to have men like these in his command. *NO!* The proper word was in his *power*. They were trained killers and he was the one who controlled them. They did his bidding. It made him feel powerful.

Tomanaga and Rossen reported, then stood at ease as Tomlin congratulated them on the success of their mission.

"By God! You caught them by the short hairs that time. Nailed three goddamned Chinese advisors in uniform. Do you know," said Tomlin, leaning over his desk, fingers under his chin, speaking to them as if letting them in on a great secret known only to the privileged few, "Do you know," he repeated, "the effect that the documents you took off of those chinks is going to have on our public relations effort Stateside? By God! It's proof positive that Red China is ac-

tively supporting the VC with field advisors
and Lord-knows-what-else. And to top it off,
all of those three men were all field-grade
officers.''

Tomlin's chest swelled up with pleasure.
"Now, I want you two boys to know how
much I appreciate your doing this for me.
You're not going to be left out. There is
enough glory in this one to go around.
Rossen, I'm putting you in for a DSC, and
Tomanaga, you're getting your second Sil-
ver Star. Now, what do you say to that?''

Tomanaga and Rossen looked at each
other, each knowing the other one would
have liked to have told the officer to shove
his awards up his ass in exchange for three
days R&R. Instead, they did the normal
thing and thanked him, at least till Rossen
saw the chart behind the Colonel. Tomlin
followed his glance and swelled an inch
wider with pride.

"You like that, huh? It was my idea.''

Rossen moved a bit closer to the chart. At
the top of the list was his correct name
along with his call sign and the number of
confirmed kills.

Tomlin continued smiling widely until he
saw the blood drain from Rossen's face. The
muscles in his jaw tightened and began to
work against each other. Suddenly he had
the feeling that he was in the sights of a

scope and the trigger slack was being taken up.

"How the fuck long has that goddamned thing been sticking up there?"

Tomlin started to protest at the tone in his subordinate's voice. Instead, he cleared his throat self-consciously, wondering what was going wrong.

"Just a couple of days, Sergeant. Why? I just thought the rest of the battalion and the world should know of you and your buddies, and of your contribution to the war effort . . . to show them how effective our sniper program has been."

Rossen froze him with a look. "You dumb, pencil-pushing son-of-a-bitch. You know what that is up there? It's a fucking commercial. Would you like odds on how many VC know all of our names by now? Want odds on how many of us are going to be alive thirty days from now? You stupid shit! That's our death warrant. They won't get us in the field. It'll be a hand grenade in our hooches, or a fifteen-year-old girl on a motorcycle with a submachinegun as we go out the gate. No goddamn wonder this war's taking so long, with idiots like you trying to run things like a fucking advertising agency."

Rossen stormed out, leaving Tomlin red-faced and sputtering at the affront given to his dignity and rank.

He looked at Tomanaga for any trace of support. The nisei just shook his head sadly, turned and followed after Rossen.

Tomlin sat down behind his desk, looking first at the door, then at his chart. *What had he done wrong?* Then it came to him. He had, like everyone else, heard a hundred briefings about security in all places. He'd even given several of them himself. Rossen was right! The clean, neatly lettered chart was a death warrant.

Hands shaking, he took it from its rack and tore it into shreds. Then, in a belated act of security awareness, he put the pieces in an olive-drab trash can and burned them. He felt very weary as he sat back in his chair and watched the pieces of the chart turn into black ash. He needed to convince himself that his error was probably not that serious. No one that worked for him would say anything. Even the Vietnamese civilians who worked around the office had been cleared by security.

Opening his desk drawer, he found a half-full bottle of Johnny Walker Red. Pouring a manly sized shot into a water tumbler, he swallowed it neat. He had always taken pride in his ability to take a stiff shot of straight whiskey and not have his eyes water.

He felt better. Rossen was just overreacting. He'd be big about the whole incident and just forget it. Snipers were a great deal like artists, temperamental cretins and subject to fits of hysteria. *Yes!* That would be the best course of action. Just forget it and say nothing more to anyone about it, and if the chart bothered the snipers, then he'd just take it down. He'd always done his best to take care of his boys.

Rossen left the camp, heading down the dirty street, which even in the dry season seemed to have gutters running with slimy mud. The ever-present odor of urine and excrement was thick in his nostrils, adding to his sense of betrayal by the fool at HQ. Ignoring the pimps and dope peddlers, who followed after the American forces like a lunch wagon, he pushed his way into the Blue Lagoon Club. It was the same as all the rest, a hastily thrown-up shack with tin sheeting for the roof and one-by-twelve un-cured planks painted in the colors a Juarez whore would have loved. The acrid stench of urine was present there, too, drifting in from the latrine in the rear. Till you got used to it, everything you drank had the taste of piss to it.

Bar girls were at their normal operating

positions, no different from the clubs in Singapore, Mexico or Hamburg, where their survival factor was based on the GI trade. The place was crowded with off-duty soldiers. Troopers from one of the Air Cavalry divisions just back from a search-and-destroy operation were doing their own estimate of the body count. A few sky jockeys sat in a corner at one of the tables made from 1x12 planks, drinking shots of Jim Beam with Beer Larue for chasers. At the bar was the normal assortment of the fine young men the US had sent over to Nam. A dope deal was being made between a Sp/5 from the hospital and a supply clerk from Ben Ket. Rossen ignored them. Pushing his way up to the bar, he ordered a double shot of bar whiskey, paying no attention to the dirty looks given him by a couple of the Sky Troopers of the Air Cav. He just really didn't give a shit.

The Viet bartender didn't like the look in the tall man's eyes. He'd been around Americans long enough to know trouble when he saw it.

One of the Sky Troopers whispered to an SFC from the 173rd Airborne Brigade, his eyes pointing at Rossen standing at the bar. Turning around to get a better look, the SFC straightened up to his full height of six-foot-three and two-hundred-twenty-odd pounds. SFC Hagerty had been on the Army boxing team for four years, and looked it. His small Irish nose had been pushed back in until it looked more like it belonged to a bulldog than a man. Scar tissue built up around the eyes and cheeks gave him a perpetual squint. He talked some more, looked back at Rossen once or twice, then grunted, making up his mind. Moving up to the bar, he leaned one arm on the counter and ordered a beer. The bartender knew he'd been right. Bringing the beer, he put some distance between that end of the bar and himself.

Tomanaga stepped inside just in time to hear the SFC speak to Rossen. "Hey, Ice Man, you kill any babies today?"

Rossen ignored him. Putting his glass back on the bar, he looked straight ahead. Hagerty tried him again when he'd failed to get a response on his first effort.

"I know all about you, killer. You got all the rest of these gutless wonders psyched out. You think you're bad because you can sit five hundred meters away and shoot some slope son-of-a-bitch in his back and then hide."

Rossen took a breath, held it, then let it out very slowly. The paratroop sergeant kept it up. "Talk to me, killer. I want to know how bad you really are." He held his fist in front of Rossen, showing off the scars and broken knuckles from a hundred or more fights. "With a telescope you're bad, but at this range I can pinch your goddamned head off before you can say shit."

Rossen let his right arm drop to his side; it wasn't a threatening move, just very easy and natural.

Hagerty put one paw on his shoulder and pushed him around.

"I'm talking to you, motherfucker! You better answer me before I rip your face off."

Hagerty's face went red, then white. His mouth opened to try and scream, but all that came from it was a whimper as tears flowed down his face.

Rossen increased the pressure of his right hand firmly between Hagerty's legs, crushing the big man's balls. Hagerty's lips pursed like a baby's as he spoke in a very tiny, pleading voice, "Please ... pleeease...."

Rossen gave his nuts one last powerful squeeze.

Hagerty's eyes rolled up into his head until only the whites slowed. Vomit started to drool out the side of his mouth as his legs went out from under him. Rossen let him drop to the floor.

From the table, the Sp/5 came up with a K-Bar in his hand, the blade held edge-up and low to his side. He knew what he was doing with a knife and he was going after Rossen's back. Rossen heard the shuffling of the specialist's feet and had started to turn to face the new threat. It wasn't necessary. Tomanaga had already moved between them, his feet streaking out like bolts of lightning. A front snap-kick knocked the knife out of the soldier's hand; then Tomanaga went into a reverse roundhouse that caught the specialist right at the point where the jawbone hinges to the skull. The Spec 5's face was suddenly out of kilter. He went down like he'd been poleaxed.

Tomanaga faced off the rest of the hostile audience. A low murmur was beginning— the kind that if permitted to grow, would mean that someone was going to get himself killed.

"Sarge, get your ass out of here before you get both of us terminated."

Rossen was still hot, but the look he got from Tomanaga made him agree. Though he didn't buddy around with Tomanaga, he respected him, and there was no reason to get the nisei in trouble on his account.

Stepping over the SFC, who had come to enough to be able to coddle his wounded crotch and moan, he moved so he was able to keep an eye on the rest of the customers.

"Okay, Tommy. Sorry about this."

"*Shimpai, nai*, Sarge. Don't sweat it. Just get out. I'll catch up to you later."

Rossen left the bar. He wasn't particularly worried about Tomanaga. The nisei had spent his entire life in the martial arts. His father had been an 8th Dan in Shotakan and Tomanaga was better than the old man, though he would never admit it.

Once Rossen was outside, Tomanaga spoke to the crowd of angry men gathering around him.

"Listen to me, you dumb shits. I did the guy a favor. If it'd been Rossen, he'd have killed him. Now back off." He added emphasis to his words by making a quick short jump forward accompanied by a piercing ki-yi scream. He brought his hand down in a *shute* knife hand-strike and broke one of the plank tables in two. The mob became instantly quiet. Pointing at the GIs with a calloused hand, he backed away, never taking his eyes from them until he, too, was clear of the bar.

CHAPTER SIX

Going straight back to the barracks reserved for the snipers, Rossen wasn't very concerned about Tomanaga's welfare. The nisei was more than capable of taking care of himself. As usual, the barracks, where twenty snipers were quartered, was nearly empty. Only three men were in the day room reading magazines and trading lies. The rest were all out on jobs. They nodded at Rossen as he passed them to go into his own room. That was one of the few benefits the specialty gave them. They had their own rooms. Or maybe it was to keep him and the other snipers away from the regular troops so they couldn't infect them with whatever it was they carried?

He was lying on his bunk when Tomanaga caught up to him.

"Rossen, you better get a grip on that temper of yours or it's going to get you killed one day." Rossen moved his feet over so Tomanaga could sit down on the edge of his bunk.

"I know that, Tommy. But sometimes that son-of-a-bitch just makes me crazy. You know what that damned chart means. All he cares about is convering his own ass to make him look good at the puzzle palace. He doesn't give a shit about you or me or any of the others. The only thing that matters is him and how many brownie-points he can score with the brass."

Tomanaga nodded his head. Rossen was right, but that wasn't going to change anything. "Look, all we can do is our best. We don't run this war and I wouldn't want to. So give me a break. Everytime you get hot, I end up getting it in the neck, too. Let's just do our time as easy as we can till we get rotated."

Rossen knew he was right, but it didn't make it any better.

"Okay, Tommy. I'll try. Now you go on and find someone else to nursemaid for a while."

Tomanaga got up, slapped Rossen on the

boot. "All right, Sarge. You just cool it.
Maybe we'll get lucky and someone will
frag Tomlin for us."

Rossen had cooled off by the time next
week when he and Tomanaga were told to
report to HQ for orders. There wasn't any
need for G2 to be present this time, so they
only had Tomlin to brief them.

"This is a pretty simple job. You're just
going out to see what you can do to slow
down nighttime traffic on the Hardballs near
Tay Ninh. You can use your own discretion
as to what targets you want to bring under
fire. Just remember, anything out there after dark is fair game. You'll pick up your
ST from one of the companies there."

Tomlin was relieved that there wasn't a
scene. He wasn't certain that he'd get off so
easy when Rossen got back and found out
what he'd have to do. But that was still a
couple of days off and he would enjoy the
break. He might even have some fun out of
it when Rossen found out that he was going
to be interviewed by a Pentagon shrink.

Heat rising in shimmering waves from
the tarmac hit him like a solid wall. Marvin
Asher had never felt anything like it, not

even on the worst of Florida's bad days. Before they landed at the strip, his underarms were already draining down his sides, turning his summer green uniform's armpits into clammy morasses.

"Captain Asher!" The hail brought him around to see an Sp/4 in jungle fatigues coming at him.

"Yes?"

"I've been sent over from Regiment to take you to the Field Hospital, sir."

Captain Asher felt a deep sense of relief. He was expected. Someone was there to take him where he was supposed to go. This was his first time in a combat zone and he felt quite lost and vulnerable. A very uncomfortable feeling. He made a note to himself to delve further into the reasons for the feelings, especially as to why he had suddenly felt so inadequate when nothing dangerous or unexpected had happened.

Gratefully he handed over custody of his B4 bag to the specialist and followed after him to where a jeep was waiting for them at the entrance to the enlarged Quonset hut that served as a terminal. To Asher, it appeared the small military airstrip was damned near as busy as O'Hare in Chicago. Enlisted men and officers alike lined up at counters, heaping equal amounts of abuse on the men behind them who were supposed to be processing their travel orders. The loudest complaints came from those who were due to be rotated back Stateside and wanted out of this place and wanted to get out now!

The faces that arrived on the plane from the States with him were different from those he saw around him now. There was a quality to them that was vaguely reminiscent of some faces and body language he had seen on the subways in New York late at night. Some had fear in their eyes and body movements; they held their jaws tight as they tried to keep control.

Others showed different nervous manifestations, their faces pale beneath sunburns, and nearly everyone was a chain smoker. Among these men there were a few faces that had a different quality to them. The jaw was set and the eyes had a higher luster to them. Their backs were very straight as they moved with obvious disdain through the others. These had a predatory aspect to them. Man, the predator! Once, in order to survive, all men had to be predators. Thousands of years of continuous refinement and education against anything violent had bred that quality out of many men. But in an unknown percentage all the signs were still there. This, or a place like this, was where they were in their element. By current standards, he knew many of them could have been judged to be functional, if not total, psychopaths.

Captain Asher was not a man who liked violence, but he had been raised on the streets of Chicago and knew how to get it on if he had to. His mother and father had worked hard to get him out of the streets and into college before he got himself killed or badly hurt. They knew that he had a good mind that would grow if they gave it the opportunity. He was on the small side, with eyes full of humor and concern. A childhood fascination with why people did things had led him into his career specialty of psychiatry. It was like constantly piecing together puzzles that were always vaguely familiar but never had exactly the same shapes, so they were ever new and exciting.

His interest in the mind and its causes and effects made him naturally very aware of himself. He believed firmly that the old adage, a healthy body equals a healthy mind, had a great deal of truth to it. That was not an absolute, of course, but many people's mental problems did derive from physical sources. Therefore, he kept his body in shape with regular bouts of handball and jogging. He knew how to box and wrestle, but they had never been more than sports to him. The fights he'd had as a kid had only been to protect himself, and he'd lost most of those. Now what he did was a game, for pleasure. . . . To those with the primal cast to them, it was great deal more than a mere sport.

On the ride over to Battalion he tried to see and feel everything at once. It was too much; there was no way for him to take in all the sensations at once—the smell, the texture of the light, and everywhere the stagnant aura of urgency, and even, yes, angry frustration.

When he'd first been called into the Surgeon General's office to meet with Colonel Baker, it had been with some sense of trepidation. Baker had never done him any favors. When he'd left the office with his travel orders in hand, he knew that Baker had once more put it to him. This was not an assignment he was going to relish. But orders were orders, and if the Army wanted him to work up a psy profile to use on those who had volunteered for sniper duty, who was he to argue? He had tried pleading that surely there were others more qualified than he to do the job. He had never even heard a shot fired in anger. How was he to evaluate fairly what kind of emotional structure would be best for a sniper? Baker couldn't have cared less.

"My dear Doctor Asher, that is exactly

why we wish you to go. You will not have any previous prejudices to cloud your judgments. Just bear in mind that the Army needs snipers. Man for man, dollar for dollar, they are the single most cost-effective weapon we can field. However, there are too many men already in the field who are not functioning to their maximum potential. There are a number of them who, we believe, are not even making hits when targets are presented. Now, we want to know why, and we want to find a way to recruit men who will not have this kind of dysfunction in the future. To help you in this, we have arranged for you to have some sessions with our current number-one sniper in Vietnam, a Sergeant named James Rossen, who has, as of this date, over sixty confirmed kills and probably that many again which were not confirmed. We want to know why he is so good at his job and others are not. It is not simply a matter of being able to shoot a rifle with great accuracy. There must be something in the personality that makes the difference."

The difference? All the way over that question had been riding him. There was always a difference in people. But perhaps Colonel Baker was right in spite of himself. He wouldn't have any prejudices built in by having had any previous experiences in Vietnam to interfere with his judgment.

He spent a major portion of his time during the flight going over a copy of Rossen's 201 file and medical history. For a man who had been in service twelve years, it was exceedingly spare. Rossen had three Purple Hearts, two from Korea and one from Vietnam. None of the wounds were such that they'd incapacitated him. He had no allergies, no major illnesses. Drank seldom and smoked less than a pack of cigarettes a week. The only complaint he had ever made was during basic training at Fort Ord, California, when he had complained of minor cramps in the right neck and shoulder when he sat in one position too long or carried a field pack. The examination had revealed no more than a thick hardened patch of tissue known as a right dorsal scoliosis, which, as Rossen had said, might be a bit uncomfortable at times, but would not hinder him.

The only information in his files that might be of value were the few comments on his childhood. Rossen had been an only child and had spent most of his formative years more or less alone. His father had died when he was seven and his mother worked, leaving him to fend for himself at an early age. He had been raised in the country in Colorado and New Mexico. He had an early familiarity with firearms and hunting, but not much in the way of formal education, having dropped out of school in the ninth grade to go to work at various jobs. There had been a few minor scrapes with the law during this time, mostly having to do with fights. Rossen was not a thief.

On entering the service in '51, he had taken and passed the high school GED test, but he had never attempted to go any farther than that with his formal education, though he had done well enough in the various schools the army had sent him to. The man had a great deal of patience and self-control. Rossen was, according to his test scores, a fairly intelligent man with a respectable, if not outstanding, IQ.

His performance evaluations from his superior officers were consistent. All stated that Rossen was a man who stayed to himself most of the time, was a bit pig-headed about how to do things, and had been known to be less than respectful to superiors if he did not respect their judgments. He had also been known to go against orders and do things his own way, something which he would probably have been court-martialed for if he hadn't been right. There was one other item that most of his evaluation reports had in common. Nearly all of his commanders had stated that if things were tough, they would want Rossen with them.

Captain Asher had no lack of imagination. By the time the plane had touched down at Ton Son Nhut, he was full of curiosity about the soldier whose code name was "Ice Man." An odd but appropriate choice. In Chicago, an Ice Man was a syndicate killer. *Had he picked the name himself or had it been assigned?*

Asher was jerked back to the present from his reflections as the jeep banged to a stop in front of what was obviously the Battalion Aid Station. Inside the one-time school house, which the army had managed to paint in its normal, putrid off-color shade of puke green, he was introduced to the senior surgeon and shown to a small room containing one standard army metal desk and two regulation steel-framed chairs. Not much, but it would do. This would be his office during the time he was to be there. Now all he had to do was wait for Sergeant Rossen to be sent to him.

He was assigned his quarters, then paid his respects to the commander of the sniper program. When he asked about Rossen, Tomlin told him he was out on a job and would be back in a day or two. Until then, Captain Asher could do as he pleased. He was not to interview any of the other snipers until after he had seen Rossen. Asher would have preferred to have gotten started right away. It would have made him feel less uncomfortable in this strange environment if he'd been able to keep busy by working. But if he had to wait, then that's what he'd do, and with as much grace as possible.

The Slick settled down on the chopper pad near the flight line, where a couple of Caribous were fueling up for an ammo drop to some Special Forces Camp in the central highlands. Once on solid ground again, Rossen just sat for minute on his haunches, looking back at the chopper as Tomanaga and the surviving members of the ST got off. They'd lost two of the four men who'd gone out with them. They'd been out on the rice-paddy dikes for two days with no contact, and then from out of nowhere a sixty-mortar round hit them, killing the two men on the security team instantly. That had been their only contact, and after that, knowing that Charlie had them located, they'd had to bug out. Something Rossen didn't much like.

"Tomanaga, let them go. I'll make out

the after-action report. There's no need to keep them around any longer."

The two survivors walked away with slow steps, stopping once to look back at Rossen and his nisei partner.

"Crazy fuckers!" They moved on, wanting only to forget the events of the last day.

Grunting with the effort it took to get back to his feet, Rossen accepted Tomanaga's hand, passing his gear to him. Weary, filthy, covered with paddy mud streaked down their faces, they waited for one of the Caribous to taxi by, then walked across the flight line. On the other side there should be a vehicle to take to them over to Regiment HQ. Neither man said anything as they crossed over the perforated steel plating in front of a hangar. A figure passed in front of them, stopped, then called after them.

"Don't you two men know anything about military courtesy?"

Tomanaga and Rossen turned to see who it was.

"What did you say?"

The Air Force Second Lieutenant moved to stand in front of them, hands on his hips.

"What did you say, *SIR?*" The lieutenant waited for them to repeat their words properly.

Rossen shrugged. It had been a bad day.

Now they had to put up with this Mickey Mouse bullshit from a second john.

Rossen moved a step closer to the lieutenant, sucking in a breath before speaking. Tomanaga watched him, knowing the warning signs.

"What did you say, sir?" Rossen repeated very slowly. The lieutenant straightened his spine a bit more as Rossen eyed him up and down. He couldn't have been much over twenty. One of those clean-cut, all-American types in heavily starched khakis and flight caps at just the right cocky angle. And no wings.

"I said, 'Don't you two men know anything about military courtesy?'"

To the lieutenant, it was obvious that the men in front of him had to be of the enlisted type. They had absolutely no class at all. It didn't make any difference where they had been; there was no excuse for their slovenly appearance and sloppy attitudes. And he was fully confident that he would get their attention.

"I don't know where you men received your training, but in case you're interested, I am entitled to a salute." He looked for any insignia of rank, and seeing none, he continued, his words dropping from his lips like carefully weighed pearls. "I am still waiting. . . ."

The muscles in Rossen's jaws started working. Tomanaga grimaced. Poor, dumb rookie. He didn't know what Rossen was going to do, but it wouldn't be soon forgotten by the lieutenant, whatever it was.

Rossen had the beginnings of a slow smile. Locking his eyes on the young officer, he said nothing, just stared. The lieutenant began to get an uneasy feeling. Enlisted men weren't suppose to do that to officers.

"So you're waiting, Lieutenant? That's good." Reaching over to Tomanaga, he groped inside one of the bags and pulled his hand back out.

The lieutenant froze. He tried to speak, but his throat wouldn't let any sounds out.

Rossen pulled the pin on the hand grenade and placed the oval piece of steel carefully, gently, in the lieutenant's hand, closing his fingers over the small bomb so they held down the handle. He put the pin in his pocket and patted the lieutenant on his cheek.

"You just go ahead and wait, *sir*. Don't let us keep you. Now, if you will excuse us, we have a previous engagement." Taking Tomanaga's arm, he walked away from the lieutenant, who was now staring at the bomb in his hand in horror. His experience with things like this had been very limited. He couldn't remember how long the fuse time was or even what model the grenade was. He was afraid to hold on to it and terrified to let go.

Tomanaga was relieved. He'd thought for a moment that Rossen was going to do something really bad to the youngster.

They cut through a hangar and found their ride waiting for them. Tomanaga put their gear in the back seat and climbed in with it. Rossen sat beside the driver.

"Tommy, you go back to the barracks. I'll take care of the rest of this. You can make your debriefing after you've had some sack time."

The driver went by the snipers' barracks and let Tomanaga off, then swung around to take Rossen over to HQ.

The Air Force lieutenant was found by a staff sergeant. He was walking very slowly around the flight line with both hands held in front of him. The sergeant had to pry the lieutenant's fingers free of the grenade, then he went over to the nearest hangar, found a small piece of wire and pushed it in the retaining-pin hole and stuck the grenade in his side pants pocket. The lieutenant hadn't moved; his face was pale and waxy, his lips trembling uncontrollably.

"What the fuck happened, Lieutenant?" The story spilled out of shaking lips in a torrent. He didn't even remind the SSGT that he had not been saluted. When he'd finished, the sergeant whistled between his lips. "You're a lucky man, Lieutenant."

"Lucky!" He nearly shrieked. "I'll have him court-martialed and sent to prison for attempted murder, that's what I'll do." The sergeant grinned at the lieutenant's discomfort.

"If I were you, I don't think I'd do that." He gave the lieutenant Rossen's current kill score and left him still standing in the same spot with, "Let it go, sir. Those guys don't really care who they kill, especially fly boys."

Reporting in to Tomlin, Rossen made his after-action report about the day's operation on the Hardballs.

"Sorry about the men you lost, Sergeant. But this is war and we have to expect some casualties to occur.

"Now I've got some good news for you. You're going to get a few days off. You know that we've been having some problems in our sniper program. The Pentagon has sent over a man to interview you, to see if we can't upgrade our recruiting and get more qualified men into it."

He didn't like the sound of it. "What kind of a man did they send and what do you mean by interview, Colonel?"

Tomlin cleared his throat. "He's a psychologist, and he's here to talk to you to see if he can find out more about snipers and how they work."

Rossen was suspicious. And still pissed off at Tomlin for his stupid charts. Besides, he didn't like the idea of anyone asking him personal questions, especially strangers. "Find someone else, Colonel. That's not for me."

Tomlin shook his head. "I didn't pick you, and you're not the only one he'll be talking to. This has come down straight from the Pentagon. It's you they want and it's you they'll have." Tomlin didn't like the look in Rossen's eyes. "Sergeant," he warned, "just remember, if you don't cooperate, your next duty assignment could be in Greenland. Face it, the Pentagon is bigger than both of us. Just do the damned thing and get it over with. And like I said, you and Tomanaga will get a few days off with time of your own. Except for the interviews, of course."

Rossen knew Tomlin was right, but he still didn't like it. Doctors were all right, but shrinks always wanted to screw around with your mind, poking and prying into things that were none of their damned business. But if he had to, he had to.

"All right, sir. I'll do it. When do I start?"

Tomlin was relieved that it had gone so

easily. Sometimes Rossen was positively mulish in his responses.

"Report to a Captain Asher at 1000 hours tomorrow, over at the 311th's Battalion Dispensary." They talked a few minutes more about the shrink and what information he might want; then Rossen got up to leave.

"Please, Sergeant Rossen ... don't make any waves. We have enough problems already."

When he got back to the snipers' barracks, Rossen looked in on Tomanaga. He was already sacked out. *Good idea!* He went on into his room. His gear was at the foot of his bed. Sitting at the foot of it, he opened all of his cases, wiped down his scopes, broke down his rifle, cleaned it, then reassembled the piece, put it and the scopes into his locker. Then he stripped, went to the shower, and hit the sack to sleep through till the next morning.

Rossen had resigned himself to meeting with the shrink. He had never talked to one before and didn't really know what was going to be asked or how what he said was going to be used. Walking over to the 311th, he couldn't shake the uneasy feeling. The privacy of his feelings and emotions had been something he had guarded jealously

ever since he'd been just a kid. He didn't
like it, but there wasn't anything he could
really do about it, except, as Tomlin had
said, get the damned thing over with. Tomlin
had told him it was important to the sniper
program and would help in eliminating
those who were not qualified before they
went through the trouble of training them
and then sending them out on an operation where they'd have a good chance of
getting themselves, and probably some
others, killed.

Inside the dispensary, he gave his name
to a PFC behind a green metal desk. The
private looked at him as if he were already
a known "crazy" and pointed down the hall.
"Second door on the left, Sarge."

Rossen nodded and went to where the
PFC had directed him. Taking off his field
cap, he knocked twice quickly, futilely hoping no one would answer.

"Come in."

Rossen had to give the door a shove before entering. Humidity had caused the wood
to swell.

He was a bit surprised. He guessed he'd
been expecting a grey beard with pince-
nez glasses standing over a leather couch
with a copy of Freud in his hands.

CHAPTER SEVEN

Captain Asher rose from his seat and extended his hand. He found that not making men who came to see him report officially often put them more at ease—especially since most of the combat types did not consider doctors of any ilk to be real soldiers.

"Come in. Sergeant Rossen, I presume."

Rossen thought, *No! Dumb shit, I'm Livingston.* Instead of saying anything, he took Asher's hand and shook it, a bit surprised at the strength in the slender fingers.

"Yes, sir. Colonel Tomlin said I was to report to you for questioning."

"Sit down, Sergeant . . . and it's not questioning. That sounds more like I'm here to do a Gestapo interrogation."

Put the subjects as much at ease as possible in the early stages to get them over their natural hesitation and resentment.

Each sized the other up. To Rossen, Asher was not what he had expected at all. The shrink was pleasant, intelligent-looking, and he didn't seem to be too pushy or arrogant.

To Asher, Rossen was almost a dinosaur— or at least a species that was near extinction or should have been. Breaking the silence, Asher began, "You know that I was against my being sent here, too, but, like you, sometimes I have to follow orders. And who knows, we may learn something of value.

"What do you think or feel about being here, Sergeant? Does it bother you to have an over-educated, non-combat shrink wanting to know all of your most secret thoughts so he can misinterpret them?"

"No more than you'd probably expect it to."

Asher made no verbal comment; instead, he took his normal refuge in the activity of lighting up a pipe and tamping the tobacco in. This gave him time to think without being obvious. *It was always important to maintain the idea that he was the one in control. Always.*

Rossen watched him closely. His life had depended too many times on what he had seen or sensed in others for him not to know what the doctor was doing.

"What's the matter, Doc? Trying to find a response?"

Asher lit his pipe, sucking on the stem, not looking directly at Rossen. *The man is very aware. He senses things quite strongly. I must be careful or I won't get a true response from him.*

The psychiatrist blew out several puffs of aromatic smoke before speaking. "You're absolutely right, Sergeant. I was looking for time to gather my thoughts. I apologize for attempting to use such a device on a man like you."

"Don't patronize me, Doctor. I may not have much in the way of formal education, but the public libraries and life were always open. Just get on with what we are supposed to be doing."

Asher began to develop a new respect for his friendly opponent, for that was what the sniper was. He had not expected this level of awareness from one who specialized in the killing of men one at a time, selectively. He chastised himself mentally for having preconceived notions. Rossen was very much aware of what was transpiring. But even that could be used.

"All right, Sergeant Rossen. From here on it will be cards on the table. I'm here to find out what makes you and men like you tick, and to see if I can put into a profile something that will enable the Army to find others like you or close enough like you that they'll be able to do the same kind of work that you do. You will not be the only one I interview, but you are probably the most important for me at this time. Also, I'd like you to know that this is not a job that I have completely reconciled myself to. I don't know if it is such a good idea to do this when you consider all the applications that our government or another one could make of this study. I'm sure that you understand there are many people in the world to whom what you do is repugnant. There is a bad taste to the very word 'sniper' that implies something unclean, hidden, secret, and evil—like a poisonous serpent. How do you feel about that?"

For the first time, Rossen showed some humor. "You're trying again, Doctor. But I guess you can't help it anymore than I can. I'll tell you this: You say that because of the manner in which I fight, I am—what did you say?—unclean. Evil, like a poisonous snake? Think about this. Do you condemn the snake for doing what is natural to its nature or only because you don't understand it?"

Asher grunted. He wasn't used to being the one who was questioned and forced into making responses. Rossen's reply held no overtones to it, neither hostile nor defensive. This was proving to be a very interesting case, not at all what he'd expected when he'd been ordered to do the job. Very interesting indeed.

"Are you saying, Sergeant, that what you do is natural for you?"

Rossen laughed softly. "That's for you to determine, isn't it?"

Asher smiled gently, pleased. *He got me again. Ending his response with another question. I wonder if he plays chess?*

"Sergeant Rossen, would you mind terribly if I tried to do my job and asked most of the questions and you give me most of the answers?"

Rossen smiled fully for the first time in ages. Asher was a likeable man, and he decided at that moment to get off his ass and stop playing games with him. Besides, he wasn't sure how long he could keep it up. He had the doctor off-balance at the start only because he caught him by surprise, but he wasn't fool enough to think he could keep it up indefinitely.

"Okay, Doc! How do we get started?"

"We already have...."

The rest of the session took on a more familiar and normal attitude. Asher chose easy questions to begin with, ones he already knew the answers to from Rossen's files. There were no aberrations in the sergeant's answers. He told the truth to each one—not volunteering very much, but he did at least respond truthfully.

Rossen began to relax a bit. Not completely; he never did that. Always he kept a part of his guard up both mentally and physically.

"Okay, Sergeant, let's get a bit heavier. Now, you just let your mind open up and say what you think or feel. If you have anything on our chest to get rid of, this is the best chance you'll have to do it. Remember, I'm a doctor and what we say here is a privileged communication.

"Now, tell me about your first kill and how did you feel when it happened?"

Rossen thought about it for a long time. It had been a long time since he'd first killed, Korea '53, with the 173rd Airborne Brigade. There had been firefights before, where he'd done his share of the shooting, but in those you usually couldn't tell for certain who got what.

"The first time, Doc? My first one that was for certain wasn't done with a rifle. It was near Chong Pyong Ri; we'd been over-run by a battalion of Chinese regular army. I'd been hit early in the fight by mortar fire and was down in a trench, unconscious. The mortar round had landed right in the trench. There were three men between me and the explosion. When the round went off, it killed them and knocked me out. I had pieces of the other men all over me. Blood covered me; my face was a swollen purple blotch and I looked dead, as dead as the other men in the trench. When the Chinese hit the line, they must have just passed over me, leaving me for dead. I came to; I don't know how long I was out. It couldn't have been more than an hour from the time the mortar barrage came in. For a time I thought I was blind. Blood had stuck my eyelids together and I was under part of a body. I still don't know whose it was. There wasn't enough left of it to identify."

Captain Asher found himself drawn into Rossen's story. Once the man began to talk freely and barriers began to come down, he had the ability to tell a story where you could almost smell and feel what he'd been through. Rossen was trying to tell the story as flatly as he could, but undertones kept creeping in, undertones that showed deep feelings kept under severe control.

Captain Asher had been in a few tight

situations in Chicago, but they were nothing like this. This was a kind of passion that was separated from crude, animalistic violence. He had to exercise some control over himself as Rossen related the rest of his story.

"When I managed to get up and clear the shit out of my brain, there was no one left alive in the trench but me. I crawled down to the machine-gun bunker on the right end of the trench and went inside. The machine-gun crew was all dead. Most of them had been shot in the backs. They must have been at their gun when the Chinese came down the trench and got them from the rear."

Rossen paused to catch his thoughts, and it was almost as though Captain Asher wasn't there. He had never talked like this before. Maybe it was good for him, to let a few things out. After all, nothing he was saying was new; it was in his records somewhere. Some of his apprehension about speaking to Asher had passed. He had the feeling that the small doctor wasn't here to put him in a bottle. He was genuinely interested, and he had said that everything that passed between them was a "privileged communication."

"You know, Doc, there's a point when you no longer have control over what you

do. I don't mean like just going mad and
frothing at the mouth. This is different. When
you are hurt bad enough, tired enough,
sometimes something opens up in you that
takes over; you just don't give a damn. You
can still think. You know what you're doing
and you can still tell the good guys from
the bad, but you just don't care what happens to you. That's when you're in a twi-
light zone, where nothing is real, not even
you."

Asher leaned forward a bit in his chair to
rest his elbows on the desk top.

"Go on, please."

"I don't know what happened next; things
went into a blur. The next thing I can really
recall is knowing that I was moving to-
wards the rear. That was where firing was
coming from. I stumbled into a shell hole
half-full of water. I don't know where I got
it, but when I started crawling out of the
hole, I had an open entrenching tool in my
right hand. A shadow fell across me and I
looked up. There was Chinese soldier standing there with a PPSH 41 submachine gun
in his hands. You know—it's one of those
ugly bastards with the drum magazine and
perforated steel jacket over the barrel?
Anyway, a flare went off, lighting up the
sky as bright as day. I got a good look at the
Chinese's face; he couldn't have been over

fifteen. He was saying something to me. I
think he was asking me to surrender. Somehow, I knew that he really didn't want to
pull the trigger. My arm shot up with the
entrenching tool in it. The blade hit him
right in the groin. He just dropped his
weapon and doubled over. When he did, I
came up again with my weight behind it
and caught him under the chin with the
point. Whoever had owned the entrenching
tool must have sharpened it to a knife's
edge. It nearly took the boy's head off. I
took his weapon and moved on to the rear.
There was some more firing. I did some of
it, but nothing that stood out enough for
me to recall. I may or may not have killed
anyone else.

"The rest of the company had pulled back
about a mile and set up a new line. I must
have just wandered through the Chinese assault force somehow. I nearly got shot by
my own people. Things went blurry again
from then till I came to back at battalion
aid. The doctors said I looked so bad with
the dried blood and guts hanging all over
me that they started to just go ahead and
just stick me in a body bag and get it over
with."

Rossen gave a small short laugh. He was
through with the story.

Asher felt drained. He looked at Rossen.

The telling had taken something out of him, too, and the graveyard humor about being put in a body bag was a defense mechanism. During the last part of Rossen's story, his eyes had taken on a distant, fogged look, as though the soul was trying to separate itself from the words coming out of the body. He gave Rossen a few minutes to settle down again.

"How did you feel about killing the Chinese boy?" he finally asked. "Was it any different from those you kill with your sniper's rifle?"

Rossen took a deep breath, his eyes cleared of the mist. "I don't really know. The feelings I have about it now may not be those I had at that moment. Time has a way of changing the past. I don't think at that moment I felt anything at all. It was more like I was just a spectator, watching someone else."

"What about your feelings on—what do they call it?—selective kill?"

"There are some who might get off on killing just for the sake of killing. I won't deny there is an excitement to it, but I think we are more like professional boxers who go into the ring; they fight, then leave the ring and the fighting behind. I don't have any compulsions to kill indiscriminately. When I do it, it has to be part of the game, and I have to believe the man needs killing or that he is going to try and kill me if he gets the chance."

"Does that mean, Sergeant, that you wouldn't kill except in a combat environment?"

"I didn't say that. What I did say was that I'm not a psycho who gets his rocks off by blowing some poor bastard away. If someone comes at me, anywhere or anytime, then he'll get what I think he deserves. It might be killing and it might not. It depends on the circumstances."

Asher relit his pipe and sucked reflectively. "You have your own kind of morality, is that it?"

Rossen was getting a little uneasy. The questions were beginning to get into areas he preferred to leave alone. "Morality? I never thought of it that way, but it could be true. Maybe I do have my own sense of honor and justice, if that's what you mean by morality."

"Sergeant Rossen, what do you feel about the Army, and what do you think about the American civilian population?"

Rossen felt better about these questions; they were straight up. "The Army is my home, and I don't think much about civilians; they're not part of my life and I'm really not very interested in them or what they do or don't do."

Captain Asher probed a bit deeper. "Do you mean that all soldiers are part of your family and you have the feeling of being a brother to them?"

That set Rossen back. The question was no longer simple. "No, sir. I don't mean that. The Army is my home, but not necessarily all the other people in it. Those I take one at a time. If they work and back me up, like, for instance, Tomanaga, my partner, does, then I'll do the same for them. If they try to bug out on me then...." He paused: "They'll deserve whatever happens to them."

Asher had the feeling that he would not want to be one who had failed Rossen.

"Just a hypothetical question, Sergeant. What would you do if the Army ordered you to fire on American civilians?"

"That would again depend on the circumstances. I know that there are a lot of people in the States who need killing, probably a lot more than here. If you mean are there any circumstances under which I'd fire on people who were born in the same country I was, the answer is yes!"

Asher ended the interview on that. He had more than enough to digest.

"That'll do for now, Sergeant Rossen. I want to thank you for taking your time and for being so direct with me. I have learned a lot today and feel that I will learn a great deal more."

Rossen got up and shook Asher's hand, again surprised at the strength in the thin, artistic fingers.

"Do you think I'm a 'crazy,' Doctor, someone who's going to go off the deep end and just start blowing people away some day?"

Asher shook his head. "Not at all. I think that I am learning about a way and a manner of life that I have not experienced before. But I don't think you're going off the deep end." He checked his watch. "I'll want to see you again when you have the time. How about day after tomorrow, same time?"

Rossen shook his head. "I can't make it then. I'm going out to do some spotting for Puff."

"Puff? What's that?"

Rossen chuckled. "Why don't you come along and see for youself? We'll be in a chopper all the way and won't set foot on the ground."

Asher was intrigued. "I may do that, Sergeant. Day after tomorrow you might just have a passenger."

PART TWO

CHAPTER EIGHT

Comrade Sharpshooter, Ngu Diem Han, waited. He knew the range to his target perfectly. Whenever possible, he had always taken strict measures of the distances he would have to shoot from. This time he had it down to the last centimeter. Where he would shoot, the road made a sharp, right-angle turn that would bring the target into his sights head-on. Adding to his advantage was a narrow ditch running across the road that had been dug by the rains. It was deep enough that it would force the lead truck of the convoy to slow down to a near stop or break its axles. Behind the lead truck came a dozen others, all loaded with supplies for the American garrison at Pleiku in the cen-

141

tral highlands. There was an APC taking point on the convoy, keeping about three hundred meters in front. He let the leading armored personnel carrier pass by; he didn't want them, only the driver of the lead supply truck. No one else mattered. The men in his security team were placed where they could give cover to his escape, if the lead APC off-loaded any men to come after him. The men of the security team were expendable; he was not. By himself he had slowed the flow of supplies to Pleiku by road to a near stop.

For the last month he had moved from one position to another, and always, when a convoy came down the road, he killed the lead driver. That was all. It was enough. After eight men had been killed, there were no shortages of volunteers to drive the second truck, but it took the threat of a court-martial or worse to get anyone in the driver's seat of the lead vehicle. Twice during that time he had taken out drivers within five minutes of their leaving their bases. One he had killed at the city limits, where the convoy was crossing over a small bridge guarded by a squad of ARVIN soldiers. The driver had leaned his head out of the cab to speak to a pretty Vietnamese girl. What he had said to her was never known—she disappeared into the crowd.

Surprise and constant success was the secret to one man being able to strike fear into the hearts of hundreds. He never failed. Every convoy equaled one kill. After he made his hit, either Ngu moved out or, in some cases, his security team would open fire from places far away from him to draw the enemy to them, while he hid in a spiderhole till the enemy passed him by. Then he'd move. Always he had his escape routes pre-planned, though there was the ever-present chance of the unexpected happening. That was when his security team was to intercede. Sometimes it was difficult for him not to take out a few more targets, but that was not his job anymore. Any additional enemy casualties would have to come from his back-up. His orders were quite clear: After making his kill he was not to expose himself to any additional danger. Twice, members of his security team had let themselves be killed in order to let him get away. But that was what they were there for—to insure that he continued to be effective.

His success had been such that there were now helicopters escorting each convoy. Blind strafing runs were made by fighter bombers, and batteries of 105 and 155mm guns randomly plastered the hillsides before a convoy departed. All for one man. But he was never where they expected him to be.

Rising up from his camouflaged spider-hole, he took the leading truck into his sights. The ten-round 7.62mm Dragunov sniper's rifle had been especially accuratized for him and even the stock tailored for his shoulder to eye length. His biggest problem was obtaining high-quality ammunition. It had taken him a long time to finally have his rounds handloaded to his own specifications, rather than relying on the standard military issues.

He never looked up when a flight of five Cobra gunships passed overhead. They would do no good. They never had.

He smiled to himself as he focused on the approaching vehicle. His Russian telescope had 4X magnification and covered a view of six degrees, as well as an illuminated distance scale and optics for infrared use. It was not as sophisticated as some of the Americans' optics, but it did what it was designed for. He concentrated on his target, a U.S. two-and-a-half-ton truck. They had attempted to protect themselves in the truck by putting up shields of steel plating on all sides and on the windscreen. They did have to leave an opening about five inches wide and ten long for the driver to see through. It would be enough.

The leading APC slowed to a near halt, as though concerned that the ditch across the road might be mined. Once over it, the armored personnel carrier picked up speed, putting some distance between itself and the rest of the convoy. The driver of the lead truck had no choice; the sides of the road bed were such that there was not enough room for him go around the ditch. He would have to slow and creep across it. Ngu could hear the truck shifting down. Tentatively, the driver set his right front tire in the ditch, gave the truck a little gas and rocked the vehicle slightly back and forth before placing the other lead tire in the trench.

Ngu held his breath, took up the slack, concentrated on his finger pull. He let his mind go in front of his sight to the opening in the steel plate. The sun was behind him, shining directly on the front of the deuce-and-a-half truck. A sparkle of light bounced back at him from the darkened cab. The driver was wearing glasses.

He fired. . . . Through the telescope, he saw blood and brains blow out of the driver's side opening in the steel protective plate, and he knew that he had scored, even before the truck came to a complete halt.

Now came the hard part—to lie still until the cursing, frightened men below him passed on by or gave up looking for him. He could hear the voices of soldiers as they off-loaded from the backs of the trucks, followed by machine-gun fire as the APC began to spray the hillside. It was dark in his spider-hole. He wished he could see what was happening. This kind of waiting was different from that when he was the hunter, and he didn't like it.

From across the valley he heard the distinct chatter of an AKM and AK47. His security team was trying to draw the enemy away from him. The enemy firing increased and he heard the crunch of a 106mm recoilless rifle shell against the wall of the opposite ridge. They had taken the bait. Give them just a minute more.

More individual fire came from both sides. The sounds of the AK and AKM were growing more distant as his security team withdrew, taking the enemy with them. He wasn't very concerned about their being caught. Struggling up the side of the mountain through the undergrowth and jungle, the Americans, with their heavy armored vests, helmets and excess equipment, were like fat beetles trying to catch cats. Only their heavy firepower was any real threat to the team. He counted off two minutes, then slid out of his spider-hole, letting the grass-tufted top back down. He slid on his belly into a nearby thicket and out the other side where he wouldn't be seen by any casual eye. Keeping low, he moved away, being careful to stay off the ridge line where he might be silhouetted.

It had gone well. Another one to his tally, which now stood at fifty-three. He had learned well when he had gone to school in Russia, where Vassili Saizevs, hero of Stalingrad and the grandmaster of Soviet Sharpshooters, had been brought out of retirement to instruct him. In East Germany he had even shot against the one they called the Siberian hunter, a sniper from the Red Guards named Skobelin, and had held his own against him, as well as the East German boy, Obergefreiter Horst Werner.

Ngu had been born in Hanoi, but he had learned to live in the hills during the war of liberation against the French when he was only a boy. He had killed before, many times. Even then he had shown a gift for accurate shooting that had brought him to the attention of General Giap. Because of this, he had been selected to go to the other Socialist countries for advanced training. He did not smoke, nor did he drink. He lived alone and, though he was admired and respected for his skill, had no true friends. Even his own comrades seemed not to want his company. They were uneasy around him. That didn't matter. He had nothing in common with them. He was, as he knew, something special, if not unique. He was a nearly perfect machine who would kill anyone who touched his weapon or his ammunition without permission. They were more important than friends, for they were the source of his power and reason for being.

Once clear of the ambush site, he still paid strict attention to the rules, taking advantage of all cover, moving with an easy grace through brush and trees, letting himself be one with his element, and it was good. It was with a sense of regret that he was leaving the valley, his hunting grounds. A few more kills and no one would ever take the lead truck down it again. But he had been sent for. From Hanoi had come the order that he was to have a special assignment, one that only he could truly appreciate—a true challenge to his skills, not this simple execution of ignorant amateurs.

On the other side of the valley an escort was waiting for him. They would take him to the Headquarters of the 246th Manh Ho regiment, where he would be briefed, and then he would wait. Waiting he understood, and wondered if the man he was going to kill understood it as well. His heart beat a little faster at the thought of the challenge. Perhaps that was what was missing from his life. He needed to find out how good he really was, needed to test himself. Maybe then he would feel complete. All he knew of his opponent was that he was considered to be one of the best, if not the best, that the Americans had.

Before this last ambush he had been given a short briefing on him by the regimental Political Officer. It amused him how the PO fumed in righteous indignation that not only had men of his own elite regiment been killed in his very backyard, but now he had to make apologies and amends to their Chinese comrades for the death of three very important men. He had personally guaranteed the safety of the Chinese, and now the only apology that would be acceptable was the death of the man who had killed them. He had to die, and it had to be done in such a manner that there could be no doubt in anyone's mind about who had the best men. Ngu had long since gotten over being affected by revolutionary rhetoric, and the PO's reference to the spirit of socialism being Ngu's advantage over a capitalistic mercenary did not mean anything to him. Political ideologies were far in his past. He was a nationalist, but that was as far as it went. The only good thing the party had done for him was to keep the war going.

The PO's tirade against the American sniper was amusing, but it did give him some things to think about, especially the manner in which he had eliminated the Chinese cadremen and their escort. It showed him that his opponent had imagination, and though the smart thing for him to have done would have been just to kill the Chinese and then get out, he had chosen to stay and to play the game a bit differently. That was good, very good. The American was not rigid in his thinking and liked to take risks. That could work to his advantage when they finally met. What was it the Political Officer had said this killer, this *Phü Nhām's* code name was ... *Nguoi cuc bang?* The Man of Ice!

CHAPTER NINE

Rossen's next appointment with Asher had to be postponed for a while. He had wanted to see how the small shrink would react under fire. You could tell more about a man by watching him for ten minutes under fire than in twenty years of normal living. But he'd received his orders to report to Saigon for a shooting demonstration for some visiting brass hats and, while there, to take a class on new sniper intelligence-gathering procedures. He'd be staying at the SF compound on Rue le Van Duyet. He was more comfortable with the unconventional warfare soldiers than he was with the men of his own regiment. They were the only ones who never seemed to be ill at ease around him.

He would have preferred to have gone to Nha Trang, rather than Saigon, where there were at least some decent beaches. He had never decided whether or not he liked Saigon. It was full of the things most GIs loved—plenty of women and liquor and, for some, drugs and other diversions. It should have been a rest, but he never felt easy. There were just too many people in the city, and a fair number of them wanted him and all the rest of the Americans dead. You couldn't watch your back all the time. It wasn't difficult to make the decision to spend most of his off hours in the SF compound rather than go down to Tu Do street and make a night of it with "the guys." He had never been able to shake the feeling that trouble was just ahead, waiting for him. And Saigon was a prime place for it to happen.

Ever since he'd seen the chart on the Colonel's wall, he knew that his number had been drawn. The only question was when and who had drawn it. And how were they going to try and kill him?

Tomanaga was getting the last of his kit put together. As he filled his last magazine with match ammo, he hoped that maybe a few days in Saigon would do Rossen some good, though he doubted it. A call from the doorway to the sniper quarters bitched at him for taking so long.

"All right, GI. I'm coming!"

Making one last check to see that all of the gear he needed was with him, he closed the door and hustled out to the jeep waiting to take him to the chopper pad. He was to be sent in support of a battalion search-and-destroy operation this night. He'd pick up his security team from the battalion when he got there. This time he'd go solo, the lone shooter. He'd have preferred to have had another shooter with him, since Rossen was gone, but they were already out on jobs and he was it. No big deal. They'd all gone out alone before.

At the pad, an ARVIN had just finished topping off the tanks on the Hulb. He gave Tomanaga a hand with his geår as he climbed in with four replacements from the 9th Division repo-depot who were being given a lift out to the battalion. The co-pilot looked over his shoulder as Tomanaga climbed on board.

"Hey! I hear you're going hunting out at the plantation tonight. Pop one of the little bastards for me." Tomanaga said nothing as the ARVIN handed up his sniperscope case and his pack.

Once everyone was settled in, the pilot took off, the nose of his chopper leaning forward a bit as it lifted from the ass end and moved off in the mandatory whirlwind of red dust and leaves.

He was still in route when comrade Ngu was called in to report to a Major Quan Thich.

"Sit down, Comrade." The major indicated a chair of bamboo and plaited nipa palm.

"As you know from our last briefing, the man you want has, as a partner, a Japanese-American named Tomanaga. Perhaps that is the bait you will need to draw the one called Rossen out to you. We have just received a radio communication stating that the Japanese is on his way to the Americans' 304th of the 9th Division, which, at this moment, is not ten kilometers away from us. I will see that they are kept there. I have given orders for them to be engaged and contained."

"The Japanese ..." His words dripped with distaste at the name Tomanaga. The major recalled quite vividly the Japanese occupation of his country. "The Japanese will be in support of their operation this evening. He should be arriving there within the hour; then it will take him probably

another hour to get oriented and then one
more to get into the field."

Ngu nodded his head. "How will I get to
him?"

"I will have an automobile take you and
your team the first five kilometers; then
you will have to walk in. That should get
you there about an hour before sunset. You
will take your ST with you, and the commanders of each company in the area will
be instructed to give the Japanese enough
good targets that he will not be able to
refuse to take them. When he does, we'll
have a fix on his location."

Ngu knew what Quan Thich meant: A
number of his own men would be sent to
die in order to give him a shot at the
Japanese.

Lifting off nearly before Tomanaga had a
firm foot on the ground, the Huey headed
back to a safer place. Around the LZ, the
battalion had been digging in, getting ready
for a night of uncertainty. They had made
many contacts during the day, but they
hadn't been able to pin Charlie down to one
place where they could get a grip on him.
As usual, the enemy was elusive and hard
to find, until he wanted you to do it.

A temporary battalion command post had

been set up in a bomb crater left over from an old air strike. Shovels had been put to use to expand the crater into a decent-sized bunker. Trees from the surrounding forest had been cut down, then laid over the top as a makeshift log roof, with a layer of sandbags over them to give some protection against incoming mortar fire. From the CP outwards, the soldiers of the battalion had made their own shelters, and all around was the trash that seemed to collect by the ton wherever American troops congregated —candy bar and cigarette package wrappers, empty ration cans and spent brass. Tomanaga thought that the American troops had to be the sloppiest in the world. In less than an hour they could turn a perfectly good jungle, field or valley into a trash dump. Ducking his head to get under the logs, he took two steps down into the interior of the bunker. Firing apertures on all sides of the bunker were manned by semi-bored troopers leaning against M60s. The battalion CO, Major Anderson, was on the radio to one of his forward platoons that had been in constant contact with Charley during the operation and was now pinned down by mortar and rifle fire. They were only about a kilometer from the CP.

"Okay! I'll get your ass out of there before dark. I'm sending in Baker Company to

give you cover till you break contact. Once
you're in the clear, pull back to here and
report to me for orders," the CO barked.

Anderson was from the old school and
didn't like this kind of war very much. It
wasn't like the good old days when you had
fixed objectives and every time you took
one, you were that much closer to the war
ending. Here you took a hill, field or village
one day, then left it and had to go back and
take it again the next week or the next
month. It never ended; the only constant
thing about it was the body count on both
sides.

Tossing the handset back to his radio man,
he spotted Tomanaga standing in the entrance, both hands full of his gear. The CO's
eyes took in the M-14 and sight cases for
the Starlight and ART scopes. Tomanaga
was wearing faded black and green tiger-
striped fatigues, his head topped by a soft
field cap of the same pattern.

"You the shooter?" he asked, knowing the
answer before he spoke. Tomanaga nodded.

"Okay, then you get your ass on over to
Baker Company. I'll have my runner take
you there. Your ST has already been selected and they'll be waiting for you. You're
to go with Baker when they head out to get
the second platoon of Able company broke
loose. I want you to pick your own spot and

slow up any pursuit. You might have a chance, with that fancy fucking gear of yours, to take out some VC brass. That area is crawling with Dinks and I expect them to come out at us tonight from that area. I'll leave it up to your discretion as to where to set up and how long to stay. Just don't get any of my people killed out there."

Thanks a fucking lot, thought Tomanaga. *It's really big of you to let me pick out where I want to set up.*

He was dismissed with an off-hand salute and was led back into the open light by the CO's runner, Amos Kershaw, from Valdosta, Georgia, a PFC who had been assigned his present duty as a punishment by his first sergeant for giving his squad leader some back talk and going on sick call too many times—usually reporting to the dispensary just before they were to go into the field. Runners had a very high casualty ratio and the general thinking was that if someone was going to get snuffed, it might as well be someone that nobody would miss.

A muffled yell brought them to a halt. "Kershaw, you go along with the security team today. You need the experience." Kershaw's sallow face fell into pieces as the realization of what was about to happen to him registered.

The runner made no offer to help To-

managa with his gear and wasn't asked to.
Tomanaga knew what was coming down in
the man's mind, just from the expression
on his face.

From the corner of his eye, Tomanaga
thought he saw a distant sparkle of light
coming from the tree line about three hundred and fifty meters away.

Pointing to the area, he asked Kershaw,
"We got any people over there?"

"Yeah, a couple of squads with a four-
point deuce mortar."

Tomanaga never took his eyes from the
spot where he'd seen the brief sparkle of
light. As the PFC moved on ahead, Tomanaga
turned sharply off to the left where he was
behind a cluster of nipa palms and high
grass.

Kershaw, all of a sudden, noticed that he
was alone.

"Hey, where the fuck did you go?"

"Shut up and get out of the way and
don't come near me, you dumb shit."

Tomanaga rested his rifle on the stump of
a shattered nipa palm and adjusted the sight
on the ART. There he is! He took his time.
The VC in the tree wasn't going anywhere.
In the scope, he could see that the Dink had
a pair of binoculars hanging from a strap
around his neck and a walkie-talkie to his

ear. A spotter for Charlie's mortar and rocket crews?

Tomanaga settled down to judge the range and angle. There was no wind to speak of, so he wouldn't have to compensate for that. In his scope, he saw the Viet place the pair of field glasses to his eyes. Once more the flicker of light beckoned across the clearing. Tomanaga grinned. "Sorry about that."

The M14 bucked back against his shoulder. Keeping his scope on the target, he let loose a yelp of pleasure. A hell of a shot. His round had hit the Dink right in the face. The Viet's field glasses exploded as the bullet passed through them to hit the VC about an inch above the bridge of his nose, driving glass splinters into his eyes before passing out the top of his skull.

Even at that range Tomanaga could hear several cries of surprise when the Viet's body fell from the tree to land face-down, fifty feet from the 4.2 mortar crew's position.

Ngu had been radioed the information that the Japanese sniper was on site. He had also been told that the man they had observing the battalion CP had not made any more contacts since then.

He took his time, walking with ease

through the fields of rubber trees. To his left, a few 4.2 mortar rounds went off with heavy, dull, cracking thumps that shook the earth slightly. To his front, a crackle of small arms fire gave him his direction. He knew without being told that the Vietnamese observer had been killed. In a way it made him feel good. One always preferred to deal with one's peers.

Major Quan Thich had kept the pressure on the pinned-down platoon all day. It had cost him a number of casualties, but they were not excessive. He knew the normal operating procedure as well as the Americans. Tomanaga would be sent out to give cover to the withdrawing platoon. He'd take up a firing position and try to pick off the VC leaders. He'd find him; it was just a matter of time. In front of him, Ngu's team leader, a one-time dentist from Hue, led the way. He had been sent out early in the day to familiarize himself with the terrain. Behind him came Ngu, then the other three men of the ST.

Around them they saw several companies of locally recruited Bo Doi, reinforced by regular Army soldiers of North Vietnam. With them, they were bringing more mortars and heavy crew-served automatic weapons. When they saw Ngu and recognized him as a sniper, they waved in greeting and made way for him. He was an artist and they knew it.

His team leader pointed to the front. "There, Comrade. That is the most forward of our sections."

They were just out of sight in the trees. Ngu looked down a row of battered and torn rubber trees that spilled sap in dirty white, thick streams to the earth; through them he saw a wide clearing of about a hundred meters. Across it he could make out puffs of smoke rising over the trees where mortars were landing. From the Americans came a ragged response from M16s and one light machine gun. Nothing too serious.

Ngu sat down with his back to a tree. "We wait here for a time. Find and bring to me whoever is in charge of this area." Lang Thi, his ST leader, bobbed his head in compliance. The rest of the security team would stand watch to the front and rear.

Ngu rested his head against the trunk and closed his eyes. It was time to get some rest. This might take longer than one expected and even a small rest might make the difference in a millisecond's awareness. Concentrating on his breathing, he willed all of his muscles to grow loose and limp, relaxed. Taking one very deep breath, he let it out very, very slowly. Before the exhalation was complete, he was at rest. The sounds of firing were still heard by his subconscious, but his conscious mind was far away, distant. . . .

Tomanaga was introduced to the men who would make up his security team. It was about normal. Each of them had smokes in their mouths and equipment that rattled and clanked. Wearily, he ran them through the process again—forcing them to get rid of excess equipment, to fill canteens to the brim so they didn't gurgle when moving. Loose straps had to be taped down and pockets emptied. *No wonder they had a hard time sneaking up on Charlie. They could be heard coming for a hundred or more meters.*

"All right, you men, listen up. I know you don't like this kind of work, but you're stuck with it and I'm going to do my best to see that you get back alive tonight. First, no smoking. Leave all cigarettes behind. Second, no talking unless absolutely necessary and then only very soft whispers will be permitted. Stay off of the trails, and once I put you in place, stay there! It's going to be a long time before we get back, so go and take a shit or a leak—whatever you have to do, do it now. Once we leave here, you won't be able to."

The men gave him dirty looks as they

emptied their pockets, then wandered off to fill their canteens and empty their collective guts and bladders. Tomanaga stopped them for a moment longer with: "One more thing to remember: You're expendable; I'm not. If you don't do exactly as I say, I'll kill you. Now get to it and be back in ten!"

CHAPTER TEN

Tomanaga shook his head as the five men left. Two weren't over nineteen. They had the blank, eager faces of children who thought they were going on some kind of a Huckleberry Finn adventure. The only one who looked to be worth a damn was Amos White, the black Sp/5 with the M79 grenade launcher. He had the look of the streets on him. Bad streets. Now, if he'd learned anything about the bush, he'd be useful. All of a sudden he had a great craving for Rossen's taciturn company.

Kershaw joined them, carrying his gear, which looked much as Tomanaga had expected it to—sloppy. Sighing, he went over the details again and helped them tie down their gear with strips of wide, dark-green tape. He checked every man's canteen, both the standard issues and the two-quart plastic jungle ones, to make sure they were full to the brim.

"Now, listen to me. Once we start moving, no one drinks unless he drinks it all. When we get settled down, if you want one, it's okay, but till then you'll just have to suffer if you get thirsty. Okay, now, empty your pockets of everything."

Even though he'd already told them not to take anything along with them that wasn't needed, keys, coins and good-luck rabbits' feet came out of every pocket. Feeling very old, Tomanaga had them take everything back to their squad to be kept by their platoon sergeant till they got back. Once they looked right—pants legs taped down, the right camouflage paint on their faces, no loose straps or jewelry that could catch the light—he had them jump up and down in place to see how much they rattled. One more check-over and he had them as ready as he ever would.

"Okay, let's get to it." To the black trooper, he said, "Take a spot behind the point man. We move out slow and easy; watch your cover. When we get to Charley Company, stay with me. I don't want any of you people getting lost out there. It could prove fatal if you weren't where I wanted you to be."

The not-so-eager members of the ST looked at each other, worry gathering around the corners of their eyes and mouths. They had a strange feeling that they might be in more danger from the squarely built Japanese than they would be from the Cong.

It wasn't hard to find the pinned-down company; all they had to do was follow the sounds of gun and mortar fire. Leapfrogging over several rice paddies, they entered a thick patch of rubber trees planted in neat, orderly groves. Sap ran from them, thick white latex blood where flying bits of shrapnel had sliced into their thin skins. Automatic fire popped in the distance, sounding more like a string of cheap firecrackers going off than anything particularly deadly.

They had to pass down a corridor that no one held, a bottleneck where bunkers manned by hardcore NVA regulars were doing their best to keep any reinforcements from coming in. It was getting late in the day. If they held off the main American force, then the isolated company would be easy meat. Easy meat, if they'd been allowed to take it, but they had orders otherwise. Several times guns were moved off target or a hand pushed down the barrel of an AK or SKS. Tomanaga and his men were to be let through.

The commander of Charley Company had just achieved that lofty position. First Lieutenant Anthony Bochan had assumed command, as the phrase goes, when Captain Harding had gone and got his face shot off by an RPD light machine gun. Pale, sweaty-faced troops on the perimeter heard Bochan yell for Tomanaga to keep down and then order his men to put out what they thought was a brave barrage of covering fire as the sniper team ducked, dodged, and crawled their way into a grove of rubber trees, where Bochan's encircled company was waiting for them.

Bochan met them, looking at the five men and wondering just what the hell they could do that his now three-quarters strength company couldn't.

"I'm the commander here." The words still seemed a bit strange. "In fifteen minutes we're going to start pulling out. I've already got all my wounded ready to go."

Over Bochan's shoulder Tomanaga could see nearly a dozen troops with the usual assortment of wounds and bloody battle dressings on different parts of their bodies.

Two medics did what little they could for the wounded as they lay in varying degrees of shock with their jaws slack, some with vacant, pain-filled eyes. A few had anger in their eyes or indignation that something like this could have happened to them. Four were on stretchers made out of ponchos; the rest were ambulatory. A burst of fire went through the trees overhead, dropping a shower of leaves on them. The lieutenant ducked automatically.

"You'll have to tell me what you want to do. This is all kind of new to me."

Tomanaga moved his eyes from right to left, then up into the trees ahead. "You just take me to your farthest line of resistance. I'll know more then."

Bochan bobbed his head in agreement and led them between the rows of shattered trees to where his men had dug in. In front of them was a field, nearly seventy meters across, before the trees started again. Sparkles of light twinkled out at them as enemy rifle fire searched the rubber trees for targets.

"That's it, Sergeant. That clearing is all that's keeping them off our ass." A gunner with an M60 poured out half a belt through his weapon. A thin cry of pain reached them from across the clearing. The gunner spat a hunk of phlegm on the earth and grunted

contentedly to no one in particular. "That'll
keep 'em down for a minute or two."

There wasn't much choice for cover. The
terrain was all pretty much the same. Taking each of the ST people, he placed them
where they'd have some cover and clear
fields of fire. For himself he didn't pick one
certain site. This job would require that he
keep moving.

"Okay, Lieutenant, anytime you're ready.
You can start pulling your people back."

Bochan looked at the five men, feeling a
bit guilty.

"Do you want me to have the men lay
down a last barrage of heavy fire before
they pull out? Would that help you any?"

Tomanaga shook his head and wiped his
forehead with the back of his dusty hand.
"No, sir! That is the last thing I want right
now. Those people are not fools over there.
If you do that, they'll know you're bugging
out." Bochan winced at the phrase. Tommy
acted as if he hadn't noticed. "You just try
to keep their movements to a minimum and
have them move out slow and easy. No
rushing. No noise."

Looking back across the clearing, Tomanaga felt edgy, more tense than usual.
This was going too easy. Normally, the Cong
would be laying in regular mortar fire and
a whole lot more automatic weapons would

be in the game. It was as though they were laying off for some reason. Well, even if they were, it didn't change things; he'd still have to give cover. But, as soon as Charley Company had broken contact and was in the clear, he was going to get the fuck out of here. This just didn't feel right.

The Americans started their pullout. Keeping low, they used the trees for as much cover as they could get. The wounded were kept in the center as the squads began to leapfrog back. The M60 machine-gunner gave them a thumbs-up sign, grabbed his weapon, and was the last to leave. Tomanaga hated to see him go.

Major Quan came up to Ngu, whose eyes had opened bright and clear. He was rested. The ability to sleep under almost any circumstance was vital to keeping one's senses at a peak of performance.

"It is nearly time, Comrade Ngu. The Americans have started pulling back. They are trying to be quiet about it, but they are very clumsy. As per my instructions, they are receiving only harassing fire to keep them moving. The Japanese and his men are in place across the field."

"Good, Major! Then it is about time for me to go work. Remember that no one is to fire directly on the Japanese and his men but me. We must take no chances on his dying prematurely."

Ngu moved up to where he could watch the other side of the field where Tomanaga was in the plantation. Major Quan started to follow after him but was waved back. Ngu wanted to be alone—to observe, to feel his opponent, and to judge him.

Lying back in the shadows, he placed his Dragunov to his shoulder and scoped the trees, moving silently from one side of his field of view to the other. One by one, patiently, he picked out the five men of Tomanaga's security team. He could have made several easy hits, but it wasn't yet time. Through the magnification of his lens he had spotted the Japanese. Adjusting the focus brought Tomanaga's face into startling clarity. Ngu could even make out the different shades of his camouflage makeup. Then the nisei was gone. He had moved. Ngu lowered the Dargunov. He knew that if he had chosen to, he could have killed him then. But patience, as the Lord Buddha says, is a thrice-rewarded virtue. He would find him again.

Only the sniper and his men were left. Charley Company was gone. Ngu returned to Major Quan.

"Have your men move in from the flanks to cut them off from the rear. We have them where I want them. Do not let any of their people come to aid them. They must remain here." Major Quan bowed in acknowledgment and passed on the orders. In less than two minutes squads, then platoons, of Cong began to infiltrate across the path Charley Company had taken to safety. They dug in quickly, providing a wall between Tomanaga and Anderson's dug-in battalion.

It was time. There was now less than a half-hour of light left. Ngu nodded at Major Quan, who sent his aide to give the order. Three VC stepped warily out into the clearing, weapons held at the hip as they began to move slowly across the clearing. Ngu didn't look at them; he watched the trees and shadows. A dull prick of light was followed by a muffled report, and one of the Bo Doi went down. As he did, another entered the clearing, then another, none of them running or taking evasive actions as they normally would have. Their orders were to advance slowly and steadily. Another flicker of reddish light and Ngu had a fix on it. Tomanaga was firing from behind a broken rubber tree, using the stump to steady his rifle.

*　　*　　*

Kershaw couldn't stand it. Every minute it seemed more and more VC were coming into the clearing.

"Fuck this!" He slid belly-backwards away from the clearing, away from rest of these madmen who wanted to get him hurt. He hadn't volunteered for this bullshit. If they wanted to, they could send him to the stockade or court-martial his ass. Anything was better than getting your fuckin' head blown off by some gook.

Once in the clear, he rose to his feet to follow after Charley Company. None of the others saw him leave; their attention was to the front, wondering when Tomanaga was going to let them fire. This waiting was the shits. . . !

Kershaw moved at quick step at first, then as he put more distance between him and the field, his feet began to pick up speed. His legs took over from his mind; he wasn't able to stop them. He broke into a dead run, dropping his gear as he ran. His rifle fell unfired to the ground, then his webbed belt, as he undid the catch with dull fingers and let it fall by a narrow drainage ditch. Mouth open, heart pounding, he ran faster and faster. Ahead of him was the safety of the battalion. Bursting through a cluster of brush, he ran right into a VC machine-gun nest. He ran right on through them. Leap-

ing over their gun, heart in his throat, eyes
rolling wildly in terror, he broke into the
one-time open corridor that led to safety.
He had come on the Viets so fast and unex-
pectedly they never had a chance to grab at
him. His mouth opened, a scream came out
of it to ride over the trees in an animal
howl. He ran blindly to get away.

A long, hosing burst of fire from an RPD
cut his legs out from under him. His left
knee was blown completely off. His right
leg was now only a useless, shattered mass
of white bone and jellied tissue. His screams
continued, on and on, till one of the Viets in
the machine-gun nest ran forward to bash
his brains out with a rifle butt.

Tomanaga didn't take his eyes away from
the oncoming Viets as the scream to his
rear sent a shiver up his spine. He pulled
off one round, then another, each taking
their targets in the chest.

*Who the hell was screaming? Charley Com-
pany should have been safe by now*

There were getting to be too many out
there in the field. What was wrong with
them? They didn't fire back, just kept walking on straight ahead, letting him kill them.

Ngu was ready, perfectly camouflaged
with leaves and brush stuck into tufts of his

uniform to break up his outline as he picked his first target. The black man with the M79 grenade launcher. The man was half-hidden behind a tree trunk. Only his right leg was exposed to the hip. That was what he wanted. The Dragunov cracked sharply and Ngu wished that he'd had one of the noise suppressors that the Americans were equipped with. His round hit perfectly, right at the junction of the thigh and hip. There was no return scream, which didn't surprise him. When one receives a massive sudden injury, it is not uncommon for it to take some time for the shock to wear off and true pain to set in. But he knew what damage he had done.

Sp/5 White's hip was gone. The 7.62 Russian bullet had passed right through the ball socket, hitting the bone and expanding into a mushroom-shaped slug that created shock waves that rode through White's flesh like a tidal wave, ripping and hemorrhaging, turning his thigh into a thick mass of clotted black blood and jellied muscle tissue.

White stared at his leg in horror, the once black, oily sheen of his face now ashen grey under the camouflage paint. He fumbled with his battle dressing, trying to get it out of his pack to cover the sight of his mangled leg. The dressing was much too small to soak up the amount of blood welling up from severed veins and arteries.

"I'm hit" he said. "The motherfuckers have shot my leg off." The words were pronounced without feeling. It was only a simple statement of facts.

The others heard him. Martin, a terrified nineteen-year-old from Jersey, was nearest him. He scrambled up from his position to go to him. White had been his buddy since they'd been in basic training.

Ngu was ready. This was one of the weapons he had used against the Americans successfully time and again. Their sentiment. He led his target and fired. The man went down, his own left leg dangling by a thin strip of cartilage at the knee. This one screamed, and did it well. That was good; it would make the others nervous and frightened. Then they would make more mistakes. Ngu moved to another vantage point.

Tomanaga took out two more Viets, and four more stepped out into the field, advancing, as had the others, with steady, slow steps.

It was the scream of the second man that made him pause for a heart's beat before firing again and hitting another Viet in the throat. What was going on back there? Risking it, he took his eyes off the field for a moment and saw the man who had tried to reach White rolling around on the ground, screaming and crying. Blood welled up from between his fingers as he tried to keep his leg from falling off by holding on to it.

In spite of orders for silence, one of the remaining two men yelled at Tomanaga. "Hey, son-of-a-bitch, they got a sniper of their own out there and he's done hit White and Martin. You better find him and get him off our ass before he kills all of us!"

Tomanaga still didn't understand what was taking place, but he knew it was something bad.

"Fuck this! Open fire and get the hell out of here. I'll give you cover till you get White and the others away."

They did as they were ordered, each man emptying a full magazine at the silent approaching Viets. Then they broke and ran, each going to one of the downed men. White was as pale as dry dust. He was dying. Nearly all of his body's blood had drained from him, soaking the earth in a dark, thick pool. His heart was fluttering as the pressure in his veins and arteries lessened to the point where they could not stay open. He lifted his eyes to look up at the dark figure standing over him, raised his hand as though trying to expound on something terribly profound, then died.

The man looked down at White and threw up, then ran to try and help with the other wounded man. The two survivors looked at each other, then at Martin screaming at their feet. They knew their odds on getting out alive would be cut drastically if they had to haul him with them. Neither had the guts to put a bullet into the brain of the screaming soldier and leave him. Each grabbed an arm and hauled him to his feet, ignoring his cries of pain. They ran, dragging him between them, paying no attention to each new outburst of pain as they ran through brush or dragged his wounded leg over brush and tree stumps.

Tomanaga moved from his cover, firing as he went. He didn't take much time with his shots, just aimed for the biggest part of the body and went on to the next one. Why weren't they firing at him? There was some shooting going on, but it was coming from his rear. Something was very, fucking wrong!

Martin lay face up, his wrecked leg twisted under his body. To either side of him the other Americans lay dead. He wanted to make some kind of protest, to tell the small, dark men gathering around him that he was ready to surrender, that he wouldn't hurt them. Before his tongue could find the words, it was split by the cold steel. The triangular-shaped spike, a made-in-China bayonet, went through his tongue, forcing it back into his palate, then pushed on into the bone at the base of his skull. Martin still tried to make them understand that he wasn't their enemy as the blade, poking out of the base of his skull, twisted back and forth. He could hear the sounds of his skull bones squeaking as they were amplified by his cranial cavity and transmitted to his eardrums. He had the brief knowledge that something in front of his eyes had flashed. The VC with the bayonet tired of trying to force the long spike back out; it was stuck and he was in a hurry. So he did the simplest and most obvious thing; he fired one shot into the American's open mouth to free his weapon from the confining bone.

Ngu gave Major Quan permission to have his men fire, as long as they aimed high. He wanted only enough covering fire to be able to get across the field. The Japanese was now alone.

*   *   *

The enemy side of the clearing broke open,
and hundreds of rounds burst from every
bush and tree. Branches and leaves rained
down on Tomanaga as he hit the deck, thinking it was a miracle that he hadn't been hit.

Ngu moved with care, not too rushed, not
too slow, his body taking advantage of every dip and shadow, of every thin cluster of
grass. He was across the clearing and in the
trees with Tomanaga. He didn't wait there,
but went on behind the Japanese, taking
the path he knew the nisei would have to
use. The man hadn't been in there long
enough to try another way. He would go
out the same way he was brought in.

The firing abruptly halted. Tomanaga rose
back to his knees ready to fire. Nothing! All
of the Viets had hit the deck and were silent.
They just lay there on the field, crawling on
their bellies through the wounded and the
dead. *Why had they quit?*

He didn't want to hang around and find
out. This shit was getting spooky. Backing
away, he took his gear with him. The shadows were long now, the sun was almost

down. Tomanaga resisted the desire to move too fast; any noise at all could give him away. On all sides of the trees he could hear people moving. The Viets were all around him, closing in. He had only one way to go and that was the way he had come in. His concentration was on the trail ahead as he passed over the litter left behind by Charley Company.

A heavy machine gun came into play up ahead. A Russian one! That was good. If there was some firing up ahead, then it meant he was close to the battalion's line. If he could just keep ahead of the Dinks or stay hidden from them till dark, he'd have a chance. He was still thinking about having a chance when a bush rose up out of the ground right in front of him. The world went sparkling in a kaleidoscope of lights, then dimmed and went to silent black.

Ngu stood over Tomanaga's body. The Japanese's jaw looked like it was fractured from the butt stroke Ngu had given him with his Dragunov. It had gone quite well. He had the bait he needed to get the *Phü Nhäm* to come to him. All it had required was a bit of patience and foresight.

CHAPTER ELEVEN

Rossen was uneasy. He still couldn't get over the loss of Tommy. Death he could deal with. It was expected, even natural. But to be missing—that was a horror! Tomanaga was too good just to be taken. He knew that the nisei, like him, had long before come to the conclusion that if they were in danger of being captured and they were able to, they'd kill themselves. Tomanaga never left his mind on the flight back from Saigon. He'd raised so much hell there that they let him off the demonstration and brought in another shooter to handle it. He'd tried to get permission to go back into the rubber plantation and search for Tomanaga's body. Colonel Tomlin showed him the report from a Colonel Anderson whose men had gone back into the plantation the next day and had found the bodies of Tommy's ST, but swore there was no sign of the nisei.

Tomlin was glad there was a shrink on hand. Rossen was so damned testy about everything that he wasn't fit to go back into the field and he needed every man he had. Maybe Captain Asher could settle him down a bit. He gave Rossen a direct order to continue with the interviews.

Asher concentrated again on getting Rossen to talk. He could feel that there was a need in the man to let things out, especially with the loss of Tomanaga. Asher thought that maybe Rossen had a friend but didn't know it. He wanted to help Rossen, but he knew he couldn't let him know that he was doing it. Any help he gave Rossen would have to be hidden beneath their formal interviews.

A problem never has its cause at the end; therefore, you had to go back to the beginnings. A knock at his door signaled that it was time to get on with the job.

"Come in, Sergeant."

Rossen sat down heavily, looking very tired, his shoulders sloping; the manner in which his hands hung limp between his legs

. . . everything an indication of the concern he had for Tomanaga.

"Please believe me, Sergeant, when I say how sorry I am to hear about your friend." He used the word friend casually, but on purpose. Lighting up a fresh pipe, he puffed out a cloud of smoke and pointed the stem at Rossen. "I know this is not a good time for you, but we still have a job to do. Is that all right with you?"

Rossen nodded his head. He really didn't care much what he did right now, and he didn't know why.

Asher leaned back in his chair and re-capped briefly their first talk, then urged Rossen to get back on the subject of his first kill as a sniper. He felt that this was a vital element and had to be brought out.

Rossen began to talk, this time telling his story more as if he were giving the Regimental Intelligence Officer an after-action report. His eyes grew hazy again.

"On March 8th, at 1910 hours, with the 3rd of the 60th, we were inserted with another company to reinforce the one who had been conducting a recon in force. Me and my back-up hit on a cold LZ and had moved through the company already on the ground. The terrain was very heavy, with dense foliage and a lot of bamboo, not leaving us much in the way of having any clear fire areas. As we were passing through the recon company, we began to take fire. I don't know how many VC were out there, but it sounded like perhaps a platoon was in contact with us. I hit the ground when fire broke out and went into a low crawl. We were on a wide rice dike or, as we call them, a Hardball. I took cover, and then, when things settled down, I looked around for a place where I could do some shooting. I found a spot about three or four hundred meters deep, something like an alley between the trees and bamboo. I took up a position and watched this alley between the heavy growth.

"After about two hours a single Dink moved into the clear zone. I should have used the night scope; it was getting pretty dark, but I smoked him anyway. This was the first time I saw just what I could do with the M14 shooting match loads. Even though the scope was only set on three power, I saw quite clearly what the effects of the hit were on the man's body. The round picked him up like a rag doll and literally blew him off of his feet.

"The reaction afterwards was something totally unexpected. I found myself shaking, nearly sick to my stomach. There was only the one contact that night and only the one kill made. It bothered me all that night and

I wasn't sure that I would be able to do it again. This wasn't war; it was assassination, murder. I went on a number of different assignments after that and always I had the same reactions. I don't know how many people I killed, but it was becoming more and more difficult to pull the trigger. When I finally caught myself pulling deliberately off of the target, I knew that I was getting into trouble and had to force myself to let him hold one.

"After that action was over, I had a long talk with a Major Wyatt and told him about it and how I felt. Major Wyatt, who was in charge of the program at that time, told me that I had all the attributes that were required to do the job and it was up to me to decide if I could continue or not. But I was to remember that I was also saving the lives of a lot of Americans. Every Viet Cong I took out was one who would not be able to fight anymore.

"He gave me three days' R&R and I went to Singapore. There I found out my answer. I did a lot of soul-searching and tested myself. When I came back, I knew I wouldn't have the same problem again. I would be able to function and separate myself from the killings. From that time on I have never had any adverse problems when I smoked one."

The haze lifted from his eyes again. Asher was finding out new things about this strange, normally silent man, things that had a disturbing effect on him.

"What did you do in Singapore that brought you around to this way of thinking and the change in your attitude?"

Rossen rose to his feet. "I told you, Doc. I tested myself."

Asher knew the interview was over. He would get no more from Rossen this day, and wasn't certain he even wanted to. After Rossen left and he was alone, he began to formulate his initial report. Using a tape recorder, from which he'd transcribe later, he gave his impressions.

"The subject is a white male in good physical health. He is a man who has isolated himself from most of society. I think that the source of this comes from the early death of his father, which he resents but has never acknowledged. He feels his father let him down, betrayed him, by dying and leaving him alone to be raised by his mother, who never had much time for him and was not a proper substitute for the strong father-figure he needed.

"He spent much of his early years living by himself. Example: When he was only eleven or twelve, during school vacations, he would take a rifle, go out to the mountains and live by himself for one or two months at a time without having any other human contact. This gave him a feeling of being independent or, as he would put it, being in control. That is a subject which he returns to many times. Being in control, to him, I think, means both never being hurt or disappointed. If you don't create friends or fall in love, then they can't hurt you.

"He is alert, and I find no psychotic tendencies in him at this juncture. In conclusion, he is very lonely, a hollow man, who has tried to make the Army his surrogate family and who has not completely succeeded in doing that. He keeps everything inside him and allows no one to get very close. This is probably the first time in his life that he has ever spoken about himself in any detail. The fact that he is talking freely to me is a good sign that there is hope that he will be able to make the emotional adjustments needed to function in a more conventional society. But, if he ever loses the environment he needs to have an identity, or if he feels that the Army or, in the event of his separation from service, that society has betrayed him, I would not care to venture any speculation on what his actions might be.

"I have not yet seen the man in action, but I still want to go out with him on what he calls a spotting run. I do know this: He is without a doubt one of the most dangerous men in existence today.

"I can only hope that we are to be able to have further talks and perhaps he will come out of his shell a bit more. However, if that happens, I do not know if he will be able to continue in his present specialty. He is not the only one I have interviewed from among the successful snipers who have many of these same problems.

"I reiterate: What will become of these men when they are no longer needed by our Army and they are cast out? For that is what some of them will feel—*cast out.* I strongly recommend that a follow-up program be instituted to track their progress for some years after their separation from service or their return to the States. Many of them will need a great deal of help in readjusting their lives to fit a more conventional mold. Unfortunately, there will be some of them who will not be able to make that adjustment. We can only wait and watch to see what we will have let loose on the world.

"Some of these hollow men will find something violent to fill their lives with, and I would not wish to be within telescope range of them when they do."

Asher turned off the recorder. He felt

drained, angry that he wasn't able to give the man a magic pill that would bring him back to the other world, for the one he walked in was terrible—not only in what he did in it, but what it was doing to him. Every day he was isolating himself farther and farther from humanity, and if it didn't stop, the day would come when he would no longer be human anymore. Just a killing machine. And the loss of Tomanaga only added to that possibility. That was another rejection for him, another failure of someone he cared for to survive and stay with him. . . .

Bullshit! He stormed out of the office and headed for the Officers' Club. He needed a drink, and needed it now. The prescription was a bit old-fashioned in this age of wonder chemicals and personality-altering drugs, but sometimes the old ways were best, or at least more satisfying.

The Officers' Club was one of those marvelous structures the Engineers threw up overnight. Tin sheeting and wood. It was crowded, as usual. Here there was never a shortage of customers.

Asher pushed his way through the throng of camouflage fatigues and flight suits to find a small table, made from one of the large spindles they used to wrap telephone cables on, and sat down in a native-made rattan chair. It was the only empty table. He watched the bar and wondered why it was that most men who came into a saloon alone preferred to stand at the bar rather than take a comfortable seat to drink.

A Vietnamese waiter took his order for a double scotch and water. Asher began to wonder why he'd come here rather than go to his quarters and have his drink in private. Someone had put a country-and-western tape on the Sony stereo and some tinny-toned redneck or other was singing about cheating and drinking. But, then, all country songs were about cheating and drinking.

Behind him, hanging on the wall, was a Chi-com SKS and a VC red and blue flag with a gold star in the center. Similar trophies decorated the other walls around the club, along with fly-specked, undusted pictures of past commanders who hung side-by-side, eternally grey, in neat, unseen rows by the latrine.

"Mind if I join you, Doctor?"

Asher looked up. Colonel Tomlin stood there, smug and neat in double-starched khakis with razor creases in his trousers that were bloused into jump boots. Asher noticed he wasn't wearing paratroop wings.

"Why not?" He pointed to the other empty chair. Tomlin sat down, grunting heavily with the effort as he did so. The Viet waiter brought Asher his drink and Tomlin ordered a Jim Beam on the rocks.

"How's it going, Doc? You find out yet what makes my people tick? I'll tell you the truth; I'm in charge of them and I can't do it. All I can tell you is that they're all fucking prima donnas who think this war can't be run without them."

He leaned over in a conspiratorial manner and whispered, "I'll tell you something else. Rossen is the worst of the lot. Sometimes I think he's just a hair away from blowing my ass off."

It was hard for Asher to resist saying, "Well, at least that might help our war effort a bit."

Tomlin's drink came and he paid the waiter in funny money, scrip, insisting on covering Asher's drink, too.

"Look, Doctor, I'm on your side. I need for you to do a good job. If you can find out what makes these sons-a-bitches work, and a way to weed out those who can't cut it, I could double or triple our sniper program and put some damned muscle into the field. A good sniper is worth his weight in gold."

Asher took a pull at his drink and winced as the ice-cold whisky hit him between the eyes. He waited for the pain to pass.

"Colonel Tomlin, have you ever thought about what's going to happen to these men when the Army is through with them and turns them loose on the streets."

"No, why?"

Asher cringed. *My God, is the whole damned world filled with cretins?* "Because, Colonel, I believe there is every possibility that when some of those men go out in the cold, someone or something is going to make them snap and they'll fight back the only way they know how. Maybe one of them will just climb on top of a building or a water tower one day and see how many people he can kill."

Tomlin put his glass back on the table. "Who gives a shit? I need more snipers now. What the fuck do I care if one or two of them go off the deep end and waste a few civilians? Hell, we're over-populated now." Tomlin laughed and snorted at his joke. "Shit, Doctor, maybe I can start up a company for them when they get out. A pest-removal service. There's plenty of shit on our own streets that needs cleaning up."

Asher felt ill. The drink in his stomach had turned to sour bile that threatened to come pouring out of his mouth. *Good God! Is this the kind of minds we have running the Army? He really doesn't care if some of his men get out and go on a killing binge just as long as he can use them now.*

It took a lot of effort for Asher to keep his

hands off Tomlin's throat. "You know, Colonel, maybe you and I should have a couple of sessions."

Tomlin waved at the waiter to bring another round. "Why? There's nothing wrong with me. It's those crazy shooters you're here to check out."

Asher couldn't resist it. "I know, Colonel, but I just want you to know that I'm here to help. Your problem might possibly be cured with proper consultation."

Tomlin forgot about drinking. "What problem? I don't have any problems."

Asher put on his best, confidential, know-everything voice. "You know, Colonel, it's not something to discuss where other ears might hear us, but I just want you to know that I will be available when you want to talk about it."

Asher left him sitting there, eyes worried, brow furrowed and concerned, both his hands in a white-knuckled death grip on his drink.

There were a few times when being a shrink had fringe benefits to it. He had no idea of what problems Tomlin might have, and now Tomlin wasn't sure. If he was any judge, Tomlin would start to worry himself sick about what his problem was and how did Asher know about it. If Tomlin didn't have a problem now, he would have one soon.

CHAPTER TWELVE

Asher spent the next two days interviewing the other men on the sniper teams as they came in from the field. It wasn't a particularly time-consuming effort, as there were now only seven men left in the program. He had one more short session with Rossen, but nothing of any pertinence came from it. It was held primarily to keep Rossen in the habit of talking to him. One small piece of satisfaction that helped to break up the day's routine was the odd questioning looks on the furrowed brow of Tomlin every time the two saw each other. Asher would just nod knowingly and shake his head, as if if to say, "I'm really sorry about your problem," and then go his way, leaving Tomlin more worried than ever.

He had just finished one of these pleasant diversions when a hail stopped him at the entrance to the Officer's Club.

"Hey, Doc!"

Rossen walked over to him. "Do you still want to go up with me on a spotting job?"

Asher didn't have to think twice about it. This could be of immense value and present him with some new and original perspectives on the men he was studying in different combat environments.

"Why, yes, Sergeant Rossen, I would like to go with you very much indeed. But I'll have to clear it first with Colonel Tomlin."

"Okay, Doc. If you can go, be over at the airstrip by 1300 hours. We'll be going from there up to Kon Tum in the central highlands. We'll probably be back sometime tomorrow night. If you go, just remember to travel light—we won't be doing any formal entertaining."

Tomlin wasn't sure that Asher's going with Rossen was a proper thing to allow, but the shrink did come all the way from the Pentagon and who could tell what pull he might have there? In addition, he had been ordered by them to cooperate with the doctor. *Well, if the little shit wants to get his nuts shot off, it's no sweat off my balls. He makes me nervous anyway. I never did have much use for his type.*

Asher made a quick trip to his barracks to pick up a shaving kit and change of underwear (he had the strange feeling that he might need them), and put them in a small flight bag along with his few other personal effects that no civilized man would be found dead without. Catching a ride from an MP, he headed for the airstrip and found Rossen waiting on the runway near the tailgate of an olive-drab Caribou with its engines running.

"Well, Doc, I see you're going, so climb on board and strap your ass in."

The cargo master, a buck sergeant wearing an orange, one-piece jump suit, moved Asher up to the front of the plane and sat him down on the canvas seats, then went back to finish overseeing the loading of supplies, ammo, rations, booze and penicillin—the normal load of crap they always took on their milk runs going north to Kon Tum. This time they'd make the run in reverse, going to Kon Tum first, then backtracking to Pleiku and Cheo Reo.

Rossen handled the storing of his own gear, placing it where it was always within hand's reach. He helped Asher strap in. "Just settle back, Doc, and enjoy the trip. At least it's a bit cooler upstairs."

Taxiing to the end of the runway, the Caribou revved its motors. The pilot kept the brakes on full, till the rpms were as high as they could go without vibrating the plane to pieces; then he released them. Lurching forward, the aircraft went from zero to over a hundred miles an hour in less than twenty seconds. Its wheels were off the runway and nose pointed up as far as it could go without stalling out, something the pilot had to figure out according to the condition of the plane and weight of its cargo. Asher caught his breath; he'd never experienced a takeoff like that before. The pilot kept an eye on his gauges as he put the meat to the bird, forcing it up into its power climb, till at six hundred feet he felt safe enough to start easing it over to a more normal climb ratio.

"Wha . . .? Why did he do that?"

Rossen smiled at Asher. "To keep from getting his ass shot off. Every now and then Charlie will place some men on the glide path to take pot shots at aircraft coming and going. They don't usually hurt anything, but in the last year two planes have gone down, mainly due to nervous pilots. At any rate, the pilots just don't take any chances they don't have to."

Once the CV was in normal flight, Asher

began to enjoy it. He even ventured close to the edge of the tailgate and looked out.

"My God, this is a beautiful country!" Below him the green was so intense it nearly deadened the senses—primal forests stretching to eternity, one after the other, going in all directions. They were broken only by patches of farm land and some huge fields of elephant grass. When they entered the highlands, there were large plateaus of shorter grass where herds of water buffalo could be seen grazing. From the air it looked like a picture taken in Wyoming, except for the palm trees and bamboo forests dotting the plains. Rossen pointed out several hamlets as they flew north. "Most of those are Montagnard villages, now that we're in the highlands. There's M'nong, Cham, Bihnar, Jarai, Sedang and a hundred other sub-tribes that no one outside of here will ever know of."

Asher leaned over a bit, holding onto a line, and looked down at the tiny hamlets where cooking fires gave off thin tendrils of grey smoke to rise in the air and be whisked away.

"I've heard of them, but just what are they?"

Rossen enjoyed showing off a bit for the doctor. "They're aborigines, of some Malay extraction mostly, I think. For hundreds of

years them and the Viets have been heredi-
tary enemies."

Asher pulled back inside to where he could
hear better over the engine noise.

"But aren't they on our side?"

"They got no side but their own, Doc.
That's where the Viets are fucking up.
There's a couple of hundred thousand of
them in these mountains. Some of them
work for us, but won't have a damn thing
to do with the Viets if they can avoid it.
About the only ones they seem to like at all
are the Special Forces people who live with
them in some of those isolated hamlets.
Then, there are some who work for the Charlies because they've been promised an independent state in the mountains if they help
the VC take over from the South Vietnamese.
All they really want is to be left alone by
everyone. Poor, simple bastards!"

For one of the very few times in their
relationship, Asher heard a note of empathy
in Rossen's voice. The man's feelings were
coming closer to the surface.

"Why do you say 'poor bastards?' "

"Well, they don't have a damn thing anyone else wants, but everyone uses them to
do their dirty work and they get nothing for
it. A lot of those tribes down there haven't
reached the level of the wheel. And then we
or the Dinks come in and give them auto-

matic weapons and force them to fight for us or else they get it in the neck from both sides. And both North and South Viets hate them. Hell, they can't win, no matter who takes over!"

Rossen went silent and Asher left him alone. They were still that way when the hydraulics sounded off that the Caribou was coming in for its landing at Kon Tum. They slipped in over a high ridge of mountains to hit with a double thump, then shuddered to a stop. Again, it happened so fast it was hard to prepare for it.

A monstrous master sergeant wearing the popular tiger-stripe camos from MACV was waiting for them as they off-loaded out the open tailgate. Asher looked over the huge man: Virden stood nearly six-foot-six and weighed, conservatively, three-hundred-and-fifty pounds.

"Hey, Rossen! I'm glad they sent you. It's been a while since we went out together. Let's hope we have some luck today." He gave Asher a half-hearted, disinterested-in-his-rank salute with a hand the size of a side of beef.

"Good afternoon, Captain. We didn't know 'til just a couple of hours ago that anyone else was coming along on this trip. I'm going up with you, so I can make a firsthand report to HQ on the mission. If you'll follow me, everyone's waiting."

He led them across the field to where a flight of twenty gunboats, including five Cobras, sat waiting.

"I'll be riding with you and Rossen in this one." He pointed to a Huey with M60s mounted in each doorway and manned by two teen-age privates. The side of the chopper had kill marks on it, depicting everything from VC to straw huts, ox-carts and water buffalos. Virden saw Asher's glance.

"Don't pay no attention to that bullshit, sir. These boys just want to make sure they get credit for everything they shoot."

Virden cupped his hand over his mouth to yell out loud enough so everyone on the flight line could hear him. "All right, you people. You know the routine. Sergeant Rossen here is our shooter. When he's on to something, I'll call on your radios, so keep the fucking airways clear and keep your eyes on Rossen's tracers. This boy don't miss. We been on a couple of these together and I know. So where he shoots is where you shoot. I don't care whether you can see anything or not, because he can, and if he fires, then there is goddamned-sure something down there that needs killing. So let's load up and get to it."

Virden climbed on board first. The Huey

tilted clearly to the side when the huge man got on board. Rossen handed him his rifle and ammo, then climbed on and turned around to give Asher a hand up. He set him in the rear section, where he'd be out of the way and still be able to see out of the open door. Virden sat next to him with a headset clipped to him. The two door gunners took up their places behind their weapons and Virden gave the co-pilot, a warrant officer, the thumbs-up signal. "Let's go coon hunting, boys!"

Asher held on to his ass again as they lifted off, forming up over the strip and then heading off to the southwest. They'd had reports that two NVA Main Force regiments had been moving into the mountains just north of Highway 19 leading to Pleiku from the border with northeastern Cambodia. From there, the VC would be able to move in several different directions—south, north and east. All of which provided more than a sufficiency of prime targets. All of which would have to tie down large numbers of friendly troops in a static defense profile, if the hostile regiments weren't located and neutralized.

It was a new experience for Asher to be flying in and out of the clouds with the wind blowing in his face as he leaned out the open door and watched the earth pass beneath. The noise of the blades drowned out almost all sound, giving one, strangely enough, the feeling of silence. In the sky around them the other choppers kept pace. Like theirs, in most of them there were young, gum-chewing door gunners with long harnesses strapped to their shoulders so they could swing farther out of the helicopter doors with their M60s and not fall out.

Rossen got his gear ready. There were only two or three routes that Main Force regiments would probably take. When the Cong got that large, they'd need a good supply of water, and they also suffered from some of the same supply and transportation problems that plagued the Americans. They were supposed to have some 105 pack howitzers with them and other heavy weaponry, including anti-aircraft guns, which could make things a bit sticky once they knew they'd been spotted.

They were near the Ia Drang river valley, just skipping over the crest of a plateau that dropped rapidly off and turned into thick trees and jungle as it fell to the valley floor. Asher noticed Virden take a thick phone book out of a pack and place it securely under his heavy buttocks. He squirmed once or twice to get it set properly, then gave a sigh of relief. Asher couldn't resist yelling over the noise. "What is that for?"

Virden smiled secretly and hollered back: "Which way do you think most of the bullets are going to come at us from?" Then he pointed a sausage-sized finger down, right straight through the floor of the chopper. "A Los Angeles phone book is better protection than three flack vests, and more comfortable."

Asher had a sudden desire to acquire for himself such a valuable and practical item. When he understood the obvious logic of Virden's reply, his own thin haunches felt terribly unprotected.

Rossen connected a harness to his own shoulders, adjusted the straps, and lay on his belly as the Huey dropped over the lip of the plateau into the valley. The pilot knew his business. Not too fast, not too slow. He let his scope eye relax, not trying to focus on anything in particular, but more to feel the earth beneath and sense, rather than see, any movement. The rest of the flight kept away, not wanting to spook any VC below. They made a pass down a narrow valley at about six hundred feet above the floor, while rocky tangled precipices shot by on both sides. The ride became rougher as the Huey caught crosswinds blowing first one way, then another, as they made their pass.

Virden kept an eye on Rossen, who gave

the large man a hand-wave indicating nothing seen. Virden spoke to the pilot over his headset, and the Huey rose up and moved on to the next range to dip down and begin its sweep again. Rossen took his eye from the scope and watched, trying to open his vision to where it took in everything. They had just made a fifteen-degree bank to the starboard to follow a stream feeding into the Ia Drang when he spotted what he was looking for—a difference in the foliage below, several patches of growth that weren't as green and lush as the surrounding plant life. He smiled as he put the scope to his eye. *Charlie was getting careless. Not changing their cover frequently enough. Some of it had dried out. They should know better!*

Virden sensed that Rossen was on to something. A quick up-and-down hand signal, like those of the old cavalry days, and Virden knew he was right. Rossen pulled back inside and yelled at Virden. "I got 'em spotted; now let's pull out of here before they know it."

Virden relayed the message to the pilot, who gradually took the chopper out of the valley without making any sudden changes that would let the enemy below know they'd been targeted. Once they were back up to a safe altitude over the plateau, they rendezvoused with the rest of the flight and moved off about twenty kilometers to give the VC time to relax and get away from their triggers.

Head to head, Rossen and Virden talked. "From the size of the camouflage, I'd say we have at least one of the regiments located. But I think you better get ready for a rough one. It looks like a lot of cover has been placed high on the sides of the ridges, where, if we come down the tube, they'll be shooting down our throats."

Virden nodded his understanding. "How do you want to play it, Rossen?"

"We go in first and we go in fast. I'm only going to do this one time. You have the rest of the flight stay above and keep their eyes open for my tracers. I'll spot the guns on the valley walls first; then, if there's time, I'll lay on some targets by the river. By then it won't make no difference, because there's gonna be enough return fire from the Dinks down there for the gunboats to spot their own targets."

Asher's stomach became queasy. He was just beginning to realize what he had let himself in for, and there was no way out!

Virden relayed the word to the pilot, who passed it on to the rest of the flight, waited till he had confirmation and then gave Virden a thumbs-up signal.

Slapping Rossen on the shoulder with one

of his meathooks, Virden said, "Okay, son. It's all yours."

Asher longed for one of the nice thick telephone books.

Lying back down on the floor of the Huey, Rossen rechecked his magazine and adjusted his body to where he was nearly half out of the open door, the narrow nylon strap the only thing between him and a sudden stop on mother earth. The two door gunners did the same, patting their weapons like they were a mother's child.

Asher wondered how the others could be so calm and business-like about the whole thing. Didn't they know that in the next few minutes they could all be dead?

Rossen nodded his head up and down. Virden spoke to the pilot. Asher nearly fell out the door when the pilot screamed out over his mike, "*Eeeeeyaaa!* Let's eat some ass up, boys."

The bottom fell out of Asher's gut as the Huey dropped nose-down in a long steep slide back into the valley. He had never known that helicopters could fly so fast. They skimmed over the tops of trees as they dropped into the valley.

The crack of Rossen's rifle was odd, not as loud as he thought it would have been. Then came the accompanying heavy rattle of the M60s cutting loose as they followed

the bright burning trail of Rossen's tracers.
Expended brass blew back inside the open
doors by the hundreds as the machine guns
let loose over six hundred rounds a minute
each.

Asher knew Rossen was still firing, but
couldn't make out the single shots from his
rifle over the crashing racket of the helicopter and its machine guns. The Huey began
to buck. Not the same as before, when they'd
hit the turbulence. This was different. He
saw Virden rise up six inches off his seat,
then thump back down and knew that the
telephone book had served its purpose. Between his own feet, as he looked down, a
piece of metal flew out of the floor past his
face to lodge in the faded red nylon padding on the ceiling. He was being shot at!

From the open doorway, Rossen leaned
out as far as he could, using the strap of his
rifle to keep it from being shaken from his
grasp by the buffeting of the chopper. He
didn't have to be exactly on the mark; he
wasn't going for individual targets. As long
as the tracer was within fifty meters of where
he wanted it, he was on target. From the
earth he saw small puffs of smoke and
flashes of red reaching up for him. The pilot
went into a series of evasive maneuvers that
made it hard for him to get off his last
couple of rounds.

Then they were out of it. Less than thirty seconds had passed since they'd begun their run. Asher learned firsthand the meaning of time distortion. To him, it had seemed as if they'd never get out of that valley. Rossen handed back his rifle as he pulled his body back in from the doorway. Asher could smell the sweet, almost pungent odor of gun oil and cordite. It was oddly appealing.

Rossen sat down heavily on the canvas seats facing Asher and Virden.

"Let's go home." His job was finished; the rest of flight was now doing theirs.

They swept in over the lip of the plateau to dive and swerve, guns and rockets blasting the once-peaceful picture into an inferno. And they wouldn't be the only ones to drop death from the skies. Three B-52s had been diverted to their target and would be on site in three minutes.

From the NVA, there came a withering counter-fire. A Cobra went down, its pilot's head gone. Then another gunboat and another, gyrating wildly to the earth as their crews tried to keep some control of systems that had been shot away by anti-aircraft fire.

Virden's face was hard. He and the chopper crew were listening in to the traffic as the rest of the flight burned through the valley. Rossen knew what was happening, but Asher had a confused look on his face. Why did the rest of them seem so distant, so stern? They should be glad they got out of it alive.

Rossen caught the wondering look on Asher's face. Leaning over to face the doctor, he half-yelled, "We had the milk run, Doc. The rest of the flight is catching hell back there. Three birds are down already and there'll be more."

Now he understood. They were going away, and behind them, in the valley, their friends and comrades were dying while they were safe. Friends and comrades! Men he had never met and now somehow he felt guilty about leaving and going on to where it was safe. What was the reason for the guilt feeling? They had accomplished their mission and were supposed to leave. So why this feeling of having let your people down? His face took on the same aspect as those of the rest of the chopper's crew and passengers. He was learning, and it was something alien, something putting self-preservation into a different perspective.

Leaning out of the door, Asher looked back toward the valley. His mouth dropped open as it seemed to erupt. The B-52s were on site. He couldn't make out any of the rest of their flight, but knew they'd have to be out of the valley or they'd be destroyed by their own bombs. Then the thought hit him like a hot hammer: What of the crews that went down? Were any of them alive when their ships hit the ground? If they were, then it was almost certain that they would be dead *now*, caught in the inferno ignited by the tons of bombs falling from the bellies of the B-52s into the valley.

His eyes were watery, and he realized that he was crying. Turning his head to the side, he saw the face of the youngster on the M60. He was crying too. Tears tried to run down through the freckles on his face but were swept away by the prop blast. Asher's senses and feelings were overloaded. He was learning! More than he had expected and more than he wanted to. . . .

The heavy, earth-shaking crump of bombs faded as they pulled farther and farther away. Rossen was drained. His adrenalin high had come to a stop. Virden was writing in a small note pad, notes for his briefing when they got back to Kon Tum. No one spoke. This was not a time for barracks bravado. That would come later, over beers and whiskey. Asher understood now that the tough talk and joking was a safety valve, a release mechanism for emotion that had to be let out in some manner or other. If it was kept bottled up inside, it could eat at a man until he went mad or catatonic.

It was a silent trip back until they reached the rim of mountains circling Kon Tum. The chopper cleared by only a thousand feet.

Asher's head jerked from one side to the other. His body was whipped around, held in the seat only by the retaining straps of his seatbelt. The chopper shuddered and vibrated, careening wildly as the pilot fought for control. The freckled door gunner fell back inside, rolling on the floor. His face was gone, the jaw bone blown away. The chopper lurched sideways again and the youngster's body fell out of the door, hanging in the air under the skids, held by his long nylon strap. They'd been hit!

He didn't have time to register anything else as the pilot fought to control the fish-tailing, twisting aircraft. They were going down!

The world went dark, then exploded in spirals of light as they hit. Everything was confused. He was half in his seat and half out, leaning to his right side. The Huey had landed, but not on its skids. It was on its side in a clearing. A boot pushed against his face as he heard Rossen yell, "Get the fuck out of here!"

Somehow, in the confusion, he got free

and followed after the pilot. Not looking behind to see if anyone else was coming after him, he ran, wild-eyed, the fifty meters across a clearing to where Rossen was lying on his stomach in a small ditch cut by the rains. The sniper already had his rifle ready and was scoping out the area. The pilot was on his back, chest heaving, a forty-five automatic in his hand, the hammer at full cock. Asher dropped beside him, face-down, peering over the edge of the ditch.

Rossen never took his eye from the scope. "Did you get off a mayday?"

The pilot nodded. "Yeah. But I don't know if we were picked up or not. We could be on our own for some time."

"Anyone else in there that's still alive?"

The pilot shook his head. "My co-pilot's dead. Neck broke in the crash, and as I got out, I saw that my port-door gunner had bought it, too, and Jimmy, the freckle-faced kid, was crushed under the chopper."

"What about Virden?" The pilot shook his head. "I only got a quick look, but I know he's been hit: there was blood all over the front of him."

Asher wondered how, in the close confines of the helicopter, his mind could have shifted to where he didn't even remember seeing Virden in the scramble to get away from the fallen bird before it caught fire and exploded.

The question about Virden was answered when they heard a curse come at them from the downed chopper. "Where the fuck is everybody!!"

Rossen grunted as he lowered his rifle. "Well, it doesn't look like the thing's gonna blow up." The Huey lay on its side, rotors bent and twisted, the tail section half torn off, but there wasn't any smoke coming from it.

"We're going to have to go and get a check on Virden." He punched Asher on the shoulder. "You ready to go?"

"What? Who, me?"

"Yes, you. You're a doctor and Virden's hit. So, it's you and me, kid." To the pilot, he said, "You keep your eyes open, and if you see any Dinks, call out."

Not knowing where he found the strength, he ran crouched-over behind Rossen back to the chopper. Rossen swung up on the side and dropped down in the door. "Come on, Doc, before someone blows your ass off."

Asher scrambled quickly inside with Rossen. The port door gunner was dead, but what killed him wasn't clear. There was blood all over him and his head was at a strange angle. Virden, on the other hand, was alive and mad as hell.

"Where the fuck did you guys go? Can't you see I'm shot?"

Rossen told him to shut up and tried to get the M60 in the door loose so he could use it. A sound like that of a man's hands slapping, followed by a crack from the tree line, said that Charlie was out there. He kept working on the machine gun till he got it free and untangled a belt of ammo.

Asher bent over Virden and tried to help him get his back straightened and looked at the giant man's wound. A round had come up straight through the bottom plates of the Huey and had flattened out into a super dumdum. It had ripped all the way through Virden's right upper thigh. Asher could see the bone was completely smashed, shot in two. Probably the femoral artery had been damaged too, if not destroyed, he thought.

A rattle of small-arms fire crackled from Charlie's side of the clearing. Flat, pinging sounds on the sides of the helicopter gave speed to Asher's hands as he found the first-aid kit still hanging on the wall and opened it. He forgot his fear and worked quickly, applying a tourniquet and placing two battle dressings on the wound. That was all he could do for now, and he just hoped that Virden didn't go into shock.

Rossen put the M60 down, set his rifle to his eye and began to place careful, selective shots, taking out three Dinks. "That should slow them for a little while, but sooner or later they're going to get their shit together and eat us up if we stay here!" He looked down at Virden. "Can he move under his own power?"

Asher shook his head. "No way. The femur is completely smashed. He can't be moved."

A rattle of automatic fire from the VC settled things in Rossen's mind. "That's it then!" Not looking down, he took another shot. "Hey, Virden, what do you want me to do?"

Virden looked up at Rossen's back. "What do you mean, what do I want?"

"Well, do you want me to shoot you or do you want me to prop you up in the door with the M60 so you can take some with you before they get you? Because we're leaving and you're too damned big to carry. If we stay, then all of us die. So, what do you want to do?"

Virden rose up on his hands. "You mean you'd leave me here alone, you son-of-a-bitch!"

Rossen fired off two quick rounds and cursed. He'd missed one. "Bet your ass, Sarge. The same way you would me, if it was reversed."

Virden didn't argue that point. He came

up out of the chopper, throwing Rossen out of the way, and fell out of the open door to the ground, then took off across the field like a gazelle with bullets kicking up dust at his heels until he reached the ditch, where the pilot watched in awe as the huge man lumbered across the clearing.

Rossen slapped Asher on the shoulder. "What are you waiting for? Get going while you still can." The shrink didn't have to be asked twice.

Rossen followed, lugging the M60 and a couple of belts of ammo with him. The pilot tried to give him some cover but the .45 didn't have the range to be effective. Maybe the noise would make the Dinks hesitate long enough for Rossen to reach the ditch again.

The four lay there as Rossen set up the M60 and hosed down the broken Huey, setting the fuel tanks on fire. The chopper exploded, sending a gout of black oily smoke high into the clear mountain air.

"If anyone got your message, that should lead them to us. If not, then it'll keep the Dinks from stripping her."

The message had gotten through. Not two minutes after the pilot got off his mayday, a flight was airborne. A Slick and two Cobras spotted Rossen's signal fire and came in. The pilot contacted them on his emergency radio, which was kept in his side vest pocket. Speaking rapidly, he gave them the situation.

The Cobras came in strafing the Charlie's side of the clearing with mini-guns going full throttle. Trees disintegrated under the thousands of rounds per minute that poured out their barrels.

As the Cobras kept the VC down, the Slick landed not ten feet away from the ditch. Two crewmen jumped out to help with Virden, who suddenly was no longer able to get to his feet under his own power. Rossen was the last man in. The Slick took off, away from the clearing, and skipping over the tree tops, headed to Kon Tum, five minutes away.

The total time on the ground was fifteen minutes. . . .

CHAPTER THIRTEEN

As Asher watched the broad back of Rossen as he entered the snipers' barracks, he thought of how these men were ostracized, put away from the normal run of things, isolated and kept apart. It had to create certain attitudes in them. One would be to acquire the defensive, self-protective coloration that the feeling of being *special*, better, superior to the rest of the soldiers in the regiment or even the entire army, would give them. *Paranoid elitism.*

The other would be to gradually acquire feelings of bitterness and guilt at being left out, which would force them into an even greater sense of isolation and separation from their fellowmen. In time, that could lead to the disaster he had told Tomlin about. He'd think more on that subject later; right now, he wanted to get back to his quarters.

He punched the driver of the three-quarter-ton weapons carrier on the shoulder to get him started. He wanted a hot shower and a full night in the rack. The day's events had not been quite what he had expected. He'd have to call and check on Virden later. No matter what else had happened, when he saw the huge master sergeant get up, climb out of the helicopter and take off across the field like an over-weight gazelle, he learned something else. As a doctor, he knew that it was physically impossible for a man that large to run the way he had with the femur in his right leg blown away, not to mention the massive damage the flattened bullet had to have done to the muscle tissue. Fear was an incredible thing. He saw now why so many men were decorated for acts of bravery that were inspired by terror.

Weary from the trip back from Kon Tum, Rossen unassed from the three-quarter-ton truck outside the snipers' barracks, leaving Asher on his own. The small doctor surprised him more all the time and was gaining his respect. He'd performed pretty well out on that field. No! He had done exceptionally well for someone who'd never been under any kind of fire before. Asher was a good, steady man, one that you could count on, like Tommy had been.

He shoved the door to the barracks open, passing a mama-san taking out trash. He'd have to get on Tomlin's case about that. He'd told him before that he wanted no Viets working in or around the sniper area. Maybe if he shot one or two of them, the rest would get the idea and just stay away on their own.

The one good thing about their line of work was that they all had private quarters set apart from the rest of the regiment. Outcasts, even among what was supposed to be their own, but that was all right. He preferred being alone most of the time anyway.

Switching on the light, he checked the room over through habit before going all the way in. *One never knew.* Closing the door behind him, he dropped his gear on the floor by a metal folding chair and sat down on the edge of his bunk to take his boots off.

God, it was muggy tonight, the humidity must be three hundred fucking percent. Stripping to the waist, he turned on the ten-inch metal fan sitting atop his dresser and stood bare-chested in front of it. It was amazing how sometimes the simplest things could become an extraordinary luxury. The breeze from the vibrating fan swept back and forth over his body, sending a ripple of chills up his stomach and chest.

Tomanaga was still on his mind. He had tried hard to never let himself get close to the nisei. It had been many years since he'd let himself get close to anyone. It didn't pay. Every time he had let someone get close to him, he'd lost them, or they'd failed him in some way. Like he'd told the shrink, the only way to do things right and be in control is to be on your own. That is the *only* way you'd ever have real control over what happened to you. When you start letting others get into your life, they only drain you and disappoint you. Still, Tomanaga had been a good partner, and even if he didn't have any real friends, he still understood and felt loyalty to those that had shown the same to him.

He would miss the tough little man. He'd always been there when he was needed. Rossen knew that he'd never have to look back and see if Tomanaga was covering him. He was always there to the end. That was not a small thing. Tommy had a sense of honor and duty. Maybe it was a residue of the Japanese spirit of Bushido, though Tomanaga had never talked much about it. His answer, when asked about Japan, was to respond that he was from Fresno, even though he'd been born in Honolulu.

Rossen was getting thirsty; his body had drained itself of fluids all that day. Moving over to his bunk, he sat down on the olive-drab blanket and leaned over to open the door to his butane-operated fridge. A beer would go good now. He wished he could get Tomanaga off his mind. He didn't know if it would be better for Tommy to be dead or alive. It wasn't very likely the Cong would treat someone like him with much courtesy.

Pulling the handle on the small fridge, he opened the door wide and started to reach in . . . and froze! His hand stopped in midair, then began to shake uncontrollably. The blood drained from his face in a rush of fear and anger. Sitting on a plate in a bed of white rice, lying on its back, fingers up like a crab, was a human hand. Tomanaga's!

Rossen knew whose it was. In the palm were Tommy's dogtags. He didn't touch it. Next to the severed wrist was Tommy's HTl walkie-talkie. Rossen bent down and looked inside the fridge, checking carefully for wires or anything that might be a booby trap. The HTl was there for a purpose. If whoever put Tomanaga's hand inside the fridge had wanted him dead, they would have rigged the thing to blow when he'd first opened it. No, there was a reason for having a radio there. He picked it up and turned the switch on. Tentatively, he clicked the speak button a couple of times.

Startling in the immediacy of its response, the radio crackled into life in his hand.

"I see you've found my present, Sergeant Rossen, or as we call you, *Phü Nhãm*, killer. That is, by the way, quite a compliment. If you are receiving me, please respond."

Rossen's throat was very dry. Sucking in a deep breath to get control of himself, he pressed the talk button and put the RT to his mouth. Clearly, with no sign of the tension he felt coming through, Rossen spoke to the disembodied voice on the other end calmly, as if nothing out of the ordinary had happened.

"I read you, loud and clear."

"Good, good." The radio crackled. "I have learned much about you, Phü Nhãm, and I believe it is time that we meet. May I introduce myself? My name is Ngu Diem Han. We are in the same line of work, so to speak."

Rossen looked at the small black radio.

"I know a little bit about you, too. You're supposed to be the Cong's number-one shooter."

A pleasant, tinkling laugh came back over the receiver. "I am pleased that you have

heard of me. It will make things easier for
you to understand. Now, do not interrupt
me until I have finished. This is what I
propose. I believe that we are much the
same. Men like us have no use for politicians or abstract social ideologies. We deal
in the greatest of truths—the giving and
taking of life.

"I want you to come to me. Your partner,
Tomanaga, is very much alive and, if you
do as I ask, he will stay that way. If you do
not, then I shall send another small piece of
him to you every day till there is nothing
left of him but his agony. Come to me, that
we may play the game the way it should be
done. Between professionals. I weary of killing cattle. Consider my proposal carefully.
If you agree, say only yes, and I will see
that you get further instructions as to where
and when we shall meet."

Astonished at what had been said, Rossen
closed the fridge door, leaving Tomanaga's
hand inside. He'd take care of it later. He
sat back down on his bunk. All of this was
coming too fast. It was strange, but he didn't
really feel very angry at the voice. He knew
now why the hand had been sent to him.
Ngu wanted a trophy. He wanted to test
himself against the best. It was an intri-
guing thought. Rossen had wondered several times how he would have done against

the enemy's best on a one-to-one basis. And there was Tomanaga ... He didn't know if Ngu would keep his word or not, but there was only one way to find out. He pushed the talk switch with his thumb.

"YES!"

There was a pause on the other end, then Comrade Sharpshooter Ngu Diem Han spoke again, his words calm and measured, a pleased, slightly smug texture to them.

"Thank you, Phü Nhām. I did not think you would disappoint me. You will be contacted soon and I promise you that no further harm will come to your comrade. He is totally under my care. Until we meet, then, for the first and last time, *bon chance, mon vieux.*"

Rossen switched the radio off and lay back on his bunk, staring up at the ceiling. His heart beat a bit faster, the pulse in his temple pounding, strong and regular. He was excited. It was a different kind of excitement than that of waiting in ambush for some men to come by so you could kill them. It was a strange exhilaration, tinged with fear. Not fear of death, but of failure, of failing himself. Maybe Asher knew more than he'd given him credit for. Perhaps he did need this kind of work in order to have an identity. Meaning that without it, he would not have any real existence that he

could fit into, and any reality was better
than none.

A distant rumble of thunder broke the
silence in the room. Rain was coming.
Rossen turned off the light and listened to
the thunder. It was coming closer. He did
as he had when he was a kid in Colorado
and counted the seconds from the flashes of
light breaking through his window to the
time the thunder reached his room. The
intervals were growing shorter. The storm
was coming closer. It seemed right that it
should come at this time and the rains would
be welcome. For a time they would break
the oppressive heat of the night and the
heaviness of his thoughts. Lying back on
the army blanket, he covered his eyes with
the crook of his arm, trying to put a time-
frame on things. Tomanaga had been lost
five days ago. The severed hand showed
little sign of decay, so it must have been on
a live body in the last twenty-four hours.
When had the hand been put in his fridge,
and who had done it? A cleaning mama-san
or a houseboy? Maybe an ARVIN soldier. . . .?
There was no way to tell, but it made him
feel very vulnerable. Ever since Tomlin had
put his name and number of kills on his
damned chart and had broadcast it to the
world, he knew that sooner or later the shit
was going to come down, and now it had.

He'd have to handle this his own way. The less the front office knew about it, the better. If he let them in on it, they'd just fuck things up like they normally did. If there was going to be any chance of getting Tomanaga back, he would have to do it and it'd have to be done Comrade Ngu's way, at least for a time.

A rattle of thunder rolled over the compound, a deep ground-trembling shudder that shook the walls of the building and rattled the tin roofing under its coating of sandbags and PSP.

In the dark, he smiled. Whatever the end result, this was going to be interesting. He'd have to put himself in the mind and body of his opponent to try to figure out what made him tick. How would he respond to different actions? What motivated him? He knew several things already. First, he had to be pretty damned good or he couldn't have taken Tommy. Second, Ngu had a great deal of pride. He was arrogant and confident. That might be a chink in his armor that could be used against him. The thing he'd done with Tommy's hand was designed to shake him up, to make him nervous thinking about it and how the same thing could happen to him. Basic psy-war! Ngu was, on the surface, very confident of himself, but he wanted all the cards dealt his way in

order to have control of the scenario. *Control?*
Shit! Maybe they weren't too different. Control was the key element. Control of one's
environment, control of your own feelings
and body. He laughed out loud. He was
starting to think like Asher, maybe he had
learned something from the little man. More
than Asher was aware of. . . .

The storm broke outside. Fat drops of rain
fell to hit the dry earth in barrages that
threw up tiny clouds of dust. Soon the earth
would become saturated and slick. The war,
in this area at least, would slow down for a
time and men on both sides would wait for
the rains to pass before beginning the never-
ending process of killing each other. The
rains were an automatic Pak Time, or as
the Latins called it, siesta. Only those with
special missions to accomplish would continue the process. The rest of them would
take advantage of the storm to rest up if
they could, or curse it if they had to stay
out in it. In the dark, he watched the lightning flash and break through the skies. The
storm felt good. Somehow this night needed
a storm.

In the morning he would have to start
preparing himself. He needed to go and have
his rifle resighted and fine-tuned by the
armorer. Then he'd have to get Tomlin off
his ass for a while and make him under-

stand that he'd go on no more operations—at least not until he heard from Ngu, and he damned sure wasn't going to tell Tomlin that.

Taking his pants off, he crawled in between the thin, worn sheets of his bunk and closed his eyes. For the first time since he'd been in the country, he slept without his pistol, a round in its chamber, by his hand, for he knew he'd sleep good, that there would be no grenade tossed into his hooch this night, no assassin's bullet in his ear while he slept. It was an odd feeling to know that he was in no danger from any V.C. Comrade Ngu Diem Han had seen to that. From this time on he was an untouchable. The thought of meeting Ngu and settling things between them was oddly satisfying, as though he had at last found a reason for being what he was.

PART THREE

CHAPTER FOURTEEN

It took some doing to keep Tomlin from assigning him to another job that MACV wanted, but this was not the time for him to go out. Ngu could try and reach him at any time, and he wanted the call. He kept the HTl with him wherever he went, even when he had more talks with Asher. He'd noticed a change in the man since their flight together over the Ia Drang. Sometimes in their conversations he'd find himself asking questions that Asher had to think hard about. Their roles had modified somewhat.

Asher had indeed found certain new perspectives on men in a combat environment. He had still to answer some of the questions Rossen had put to him, such as. . . . "Do you feel any different now, Doc? I saw the look on your face out there and you were feeling the same things the rest of us were. I think you could have gotten behind a gun quite easily. And not just for self-defense. I saw something else there that I think said you kinda wished you had."

Rossen had smiled gently and remarked before leaving, "It's not easy is it, Doc? Tell you what, if the time comes that you ever pull down on someone, then come and talk to me. Then I think we'll have a lot more understanding of each other because none of it is simple. Killing is not simple. You'll find that out!"

Rossen's prophecy bothered Asher. There was a ring of truth to the sergeant's observations that Asher felt would have better been left alone. Then he realized that he had just switched places with Rossen; he had become the subject and Rossen the doctor. Grinning widely, he lit up a fresh pipe and sucked deep. "That smart son-of-a-bitch, he did it to me again. . . ."

It was three days before Comrade Ngu talked to Rossen again.

"Cam on ong, Phü Nhām?"

"I'm all right, Ngu. When do we get together?"

The radio crackled with good-humored mirth. "Don't be impatient. Everything is in order. Listen to me; then, after I finish, I will answer your questions. We will meet in four days at 1200 hours. Twenty miles due south magnetic, from your Special Forces Camp at Duc Co. There you will find a valley with a very high and narrow waterfall called the Tiger's Breath. There will be a single smoke signal to guide you in. You will know if you have missed the falls if you pass on to a large field where there is a Montagnard village that has been burned out.

"If you wish, you may bring an ST with you of four men, but no more. Set down at the face of the falls. I will be waiting for you downriver a little ways with your friend, Sergeant Tomanaga. He is still well and will remain that way. I have faith that you will find a way in which to keep our appointment. And don't forget to bring your radio.

"Now do you have any questions?"

Hitting his talk button, Rossen went over Ngu's instructions. "No questions but one: When will you let Tommy go?"

There was a pause before Ngu answered, "I thought you understood . . . you will have to kill me to save him. If you die, then so does he. I think that will give you a little more incentive. *Au revoir*, Phü Nhām. See you at lunch, four days from now!"

Rossen's next move was to make contact with Sam Benson, Tommy's chopper-pilot friend. He didn't reach him until the next day when he was passing through on his way north for a *hard rice*, ammo, drop to some Meo tribesmen in Laos.

Sam whistled between his teeth as they talked on the chopper pad. "Now listen, Rossen, I like Tommy a lot, but you're not really going in there, are you?"

"I don't have any choice unless you want to see Tommy brought back to us one piece at a time, and that bastard will do exactly as he said."

Sam leaned up against the plexiglass window assembly of his Huey's nose. "Okay, if that's the way it is, I'll take you. Now, how many are going in with you?"

"Just me, Sam. This is not going to be the time or place to have amateurs tromping around the bush like elephants. They'd just slow me up or give my position away. Besides, some of them would get themselves killed and we don't need to give the Dinks any freebies. I think that's what Ngu wants

me to do, because then I'd have to be thinking about them, too. This way, it's just me.
I'll work better then, without the additional
responsibility."

Sam just shook his head. "Okay, Sarge, if
that's how you want it, that's how it will
be. Anyway, I think I know the area he's
talking about, but I'll make a flyover tomorrow to check it out."

For the next two days Rossen was a bit
short-tempered with everyone, and most
decided, including Tomlin, just to keep out
of his way until whatever it was that was
bugging him passed. He went over his gear
a dozen times and nearly snapped the head
off another sniper who wanted to use some
of his ammo. He was going over his check-
list again when someone knocked at his door.

"Come on in."

Asher had never been in Rossen's quarters before. They were about what he expected. Spare, neat, no girlie pictures or
postcards on the walls.

"You missed out on a couple of appoint-
ments, Sergeant, so I thought I'd drop by
and see if you were okay."

Rossen started to snap at Asher, but didn't;
he knew the small man was really concerned.
When Asher asked him about the gear on

his bunk, Rossen thought about it for a moment and then decided to let him know. It would be better if someone knew the true story in case he didn't come back. Sam wouldn't be able to talk about it, because if he did, he'd get his ass busted down to private E-nothing.

When he'd finished, Asher said nothing for a long time; instead, he lit his pipe again. "Well, I guess there's nothing I can say that would make you change your mind, and I'm not sure that I should even try. I think I've learned more from you than you have from me. I still don't have the answers to all the feelings that I've experienced the last weeks and maybe I never will. So all I can say is, if you want to go, then do it! And blow that Dink bastard away!"

Asher was surprised at the vehemency of his reply. He really wanted Rossen to kill a man. He had changed.

Rossen caught a hop up to Pleiku that afternoon and stayed in the transient barracks, where he met with Sam.

"I've got it spotted for you, Sarge. I've fixed it so I can make a run south in the morning for some parts. I'll meet you on the pad at 1030 hours and we'll do it!"

*   *   *

That night Doctor Asher lay in his bunk
staring up at the dark and wondered who
was going to live or die the next day. He
knew that Rossen was very good, but he
was under a great deal of mental pressure—
that of having to save Tomanaga. Did he
feel that if he didn't do it, then he would be
the same as all those who had let him down
and disappointed him in his life? Was that
why he was going? Or was it something
else, something more obvious, yet extremely
subtle?

The earth shook. Asher sat up straight in
his bunk, *What the hell . . . ?*

Again the ground trembled, and the dull
thuds of heavy mortars striking rolled across
the compound. He got up and dressed as
fast he could, fingers suddenly all thumbs
that couldn't perform even the simple task
of pulling up a zipper with any certainty.
Another eye-searing flash lit up the sky as
brilliant orange-red clouds rose into the
night.

Oh shit, we're being attacked! From his
dresser he took out the issue forty-five given
him when he came in the country. He'd never
thought that he would actually want to put
his hands on it. The barracks next to his
burst open. A "telegraph pole," one of the

Russian-made 122mm rockets, had roared straight into it. At first no screams came from the barracks. Less than a minute passed, and Asher watched in horror as he had his real taste of the war coming to him; then came the cries and screams of men in agony.

All around him came yells for help and orders being shouted. At the dispensary, wounded men were being taken out on stretchers and loaded into ambulances to be taken to safety. Those that could walk were hustled out to sandbagged bomb shelters. Asher flung his door open and stumbled into the hallway. He didn't know where he was supposed to go, but he couldn't just stay in his room. Others rushed past him, most with weapons in their hands the same as he. All of them were medics or doctors, and they weren't supposed to be combatants. All of that seemed rather simplistic right then. He followed them outside to get in the clear.

A small figure ran in front of him and around to the side of his barracks, a bag in his hand. With a shock he realized that the man who had passed him was VC. His barracks exploded, wood splinters flying past and striking several men in front of him, but none were hurt badly enough to need immediate help. The VC was a sapper and the bag was satchel-charge tossed in the doctors' barracks. A short burst of automatic fire and then he heard curses yelling out over the increasing din of the VC attack. "Okay, we got that little bastard and if there's one, there's more, so spread out and kill anything that looks Oriental."

Men were running everywhere. From the airstrip, he saw more explosions as the fuel depot was hit by 4.2 mortars and rockets. American return fire began to go out. Artillery from a company of 105s began to fire with rhythmic precision, sending round after round into pre-sighted target areas. Around the camp perimeter, small-arms and machine-gun fire increased.

A medic Asher had seen at the dispensary stumbled past him, both hands holding his face. He was blubbering red pools of blood. He knocked him down, and forced the man's hands away from his face. Part of the lower right jaw was cleanly sliced off, as though a surgeon's scalpel had been at work. Through his wrecked face, the man hissed, "They're killing the wounded in the shelters. Help them!"

The man's wound was going to be fatal. Asher stood and looked at the forty-five in his hand. He jacked a round into the chamber and began to run for the bomb shelter. He didn't know why he was running or when he had decided to run. His body just moved. He passed dozens of men heading the other way to where a breech in the wire had been made. He heard screams getting louder and cries of pain, followed by shots.

"Oh my God, oh my God!" He ran faster, heart racing, into the opened door of the first shelter. By the glow of a single Coleman lantern, he saw no one alive. Men lay around like broken toys thrown away by a careless child. All of them were dead. The guard had been a single MP who no longer had a chest, only a gaping cavity where a full burst from an AK47 had torn him nearly in half. "Oh my God, oh my God!" He ran back out and into the next shelter. He heard cries for help. Bursting through the door, he bumped into someone who turned around, a machete-type blade in his hand dripping red. Not thinking about it, Asher pulled the trigger on the forty-five. The VC's face disappeared in a red mask as the back of his head blew out.

Asher didn't know what he was doing; he just did it. He fired again and again at small men with weapons in their hands. Several shots came back at him but none hit. One of the Viets was only wounded in the side and fell to the floor between a couple of paratroopers. They rolled out of their cots on top of the VC and beat him to death

with their hands. He shot another VC who
was trying to get his bayonet out of the
ribcage of a black corporal. The heavy, slow
slug hit the Viet right at the base of the
neck.

Then it was over. Asher stood there, heart
pounding, trying to break through his ribcage. How long had it taken? What had he
done? In less than thirty seconds he had
killed four men. *Was that all it took?* Everything was distorted, his sense of time and
space, of color and sound. During those few
minutes he had entered another dimension,
where none of the laws of nature were valid.
All at the same time, he was stunned and
exhilarated, sick and gloating at what he
had done.

Five heavily armed men entered the shelter and Asher raised his weapon. "Hey, take
it easy; we're on your side." The men went
and checked out the bodies of the dead VC.
One was sent by a buck sergeant to find
some medics to care of the wounded. Before
Asher had gotten there, the VC had killed
seven patients, holding the others at gun-
point as their comrades bayonetted or hacked
them to death with machetes.

"I'm a doctor," he told the soldiers. "Show
me how this works and I'll look after them."
He handed the sergeant one of the Viets'
AKs. The sergeant couldn't have been over

twenty, but he was no child, and as he looked
back at the face of the small psychiatrist,
he knew the doctor had done some growing
up in the last few minutes. He showed Asher
how to load the weapon and where the safety
was.

"Yeah, Doc, I think you'll be able to take
care of them, all right. We'll be back later to
clean up the trash." To the men of his fire
team, he yelled out, "Okay, you people, let's
get the fuck out of here and get back to
work. There's still a lot of those bastards
running around. Just make sure you don't
shoot any of our own men. Now move it."
As he left, he stopped at the doorway to the
shelter, turned around, came to attention
and gave Asher a bonafide highball salute,
then left.

Asher let his own hand back down. He
felt strangely good. The man had saluted
him. He'd naturally received salutes hundreds of times before, but this was the first
time he ever felt that it had been given
because the man thought he deserved it.

He stayed with his patients all that night,
taking care of them and guarding them,
staying at the entrance to the shelter with
the AK cradled comfortably across his arms,
a round in the chamber, safety off and ready
to fire. Twice the young buck sergeant came
by to check on him. He'd smile, give him a

thumbs-up sign and take off again. He felt good. Better than he'd ever felt in life. More alive, more real. Nothing he'd ever imagined had even come close to the reality of the last hours. The sounds of firing decreased as the night passed; explosions were less frequent, and most of them came from exploding fuel drums where the POL dump had taken several hits. Only rarely now did bursts of small-arms fire rattle across the compound. Overhead, choppers were in heavy evidence as they circled and swung from side to side, looking for something to kill, and he wished them good hunting. They passed on, trying to keep in contact with Charlie until a reaction force could be put together to go after them.

By the time some medics and staff doctors came to relieve him, it was full light. Leaving his charges to their care, Asher walked out into the sun. It was a bright, clear morning, even with the streams of black smoke that still boiled into the skies from the flaming fuel dump. It was a good day.

He started to return to his barracks, then remembered that he didn't have barracks anymore. His heart gave a jerk; all of his papers and reports were in the room. Then he laughed out loud. A passing APC, filled with flak-vested troops, gave him a strange look as they rumbled by on grinding treads. One touched his finger to his temple and made circles. Asher laughed again—maybe the man was right, but he didn't care. His papers were gone; now they didn't matter. He'd found a greater truth. One about himself. Everything else was diminished, and he had finally found the truth about Rossen. His analysis had been fairly correct, as far as it went. But now he knew what he had missed in his study of the sniper and why he did what he did. Asher laughed again at his own stupidity and naivete. He knew now why Rossen did what he did.

Because he liked it!

And he wished him good hunting this day!

CHAPTER FIFTEEN

Checking his watch, Ngu looked absently toward the Tiger's Breath. He had the four men of his security team around him. They had worked together for a long time. There had been some changes in them, naturally, but the *newest* member had been with him for four months. That was a long time.

Now time was drawing near for him to at last test himself completely. He knew, as most likely did Rossen, that in some ways it was a very silly thing to do. What did the Americans call it? Playing cowboys and Indians. Seeing who had the fastest draw. Childish, perhaps. But, then, are not all things only games in one manner or the other? Politics, war, life, love. . . . All only games that one must play until the end.

Now the best game of all should be getting ready to board his helicopter and come to him. This was not to be a game of strength in the sense of physical power, but one where the mind was as important as the eye. That was the reason for the taking of the Japanese. He was important only for the effect he would have on Rossen's ability to make decisions. Ngu had no moral qualms about the mental pressures he had put on his adversary. That was fair. If Rossen could have pressured him in any way, he would have done so. But, so far—and he had no intention of relinquishing his advantage—he had kept total control of the situation right down the line.

Tomanaga gave a groan. Ngu ordered one of his Bo Doi to give him water and food if he wished it. Soon it would be time to tie the Japanese to the pole prepared for him. Until then there was no reason to make him uncomfortable. Ngu had a certain admiration for the nisei. He had borne his troubles and pain well. Though it was true that he, Ngu, had seen to it there was as little pain as possible when they cut the Japanese's hand off. He was, after all, not a cruel man!

Ngu ordered his men to prepare tea. They had time; the Phü Nhām was not due to arrive for nearly two hours, and he knew he would be punctual.

A small fire was built, over which a tin pot of water was set to boil. Soon the aroma of *Cha* was wafting gently to his nostrils. He enjoyed his small luxuries when they could be had as much as he did many of his major triumphs. Now it was pleasant to rest peacefully in the cool shadows of the valley and sip hot tea and think. Think about the past and the future. He was certain that he had one. But if he did not, then it really didn't matter, for the wheel of life must turn upon itself until the cycle is complete. All must be born so that they may die. The only difference would be in what they did between birth and death.

He lay back on a soft clump of new grass to watch the skies overhead as the clouds passed gently from one side of the valley to the other. This was good. This was the best. He was savoring life to the fullest now. Every sense awake, aware. One could not appreciate life in its total beauty until one was walking hand-in-hand with death. The coming danger gave these moments a rare spice that would never come again in exactly the same way. Each of these seconds were priceless jewels to be tasted and treasured.

He half-dozed, relishing the peaceful quiet of the valley, which was broken only by the gentle rustling of the river and the more distant, roaring rush of the Tiger's Breath. He rolled over to smell the new grass. Once he had thought he would become a poet. Then he realized that flowery words could never completely relay the true feelings, tastes and sounds that one experienced. Therefore, poetry was false. At best, it could only be important to those who did not know how to live life themselves, and he was one who had chosen to live his life and it was *good!*

It was with a certain reluctance that he looked again at his watch. One hour to go. He rose to his feet, snapped his fingers for his security team to gather around.

"Prepare the Japanese; then return to me. The time is drawing close."

They did as they were ordered and took Tomanaga to his stake. Not once after their initial encounter had Ngu spoken to him. Tomanaga had only one purpose, and after that was accomplished, he no longer mattered. Ngu hadn't made his mind up whether to kill the Japanese after he had beaten the Phü Nhäm or to let him go free so that he could tell the Americans of his victory. *Ahhhhh!* That would strike terror into the hearts of many and attack their minds and confidence. Perhaps he would let him live after all. At any rate, he would make that decision later. Now he had to prepare.

Tomanaga was tied to the stake, his arms bound at the rear, at the joints of his elbows. His wrist, where his right hand had been severed, was still raw and tender. Ngu had taken him from the plantation to one of their field hospitals in Cambodia. There a Vietnamese surgeon had amputated it. The Vietnamese doctor had protested vigorously against it, but Ngu would not be denied. The only mercy shown Tomanaga was that he was given a strong local anesthetic to keep the worst of the pain down. He had still passed out when the surgeon began to cut with the bone saw.

The only time Ngu had spoken to him since was when he explained why he'd had the amputation done to him. After that, Ngu had left him alone, but he also permitted no one else to bother him. He had been treated well enough by Asian standards. He was watered, fed and ignored. He had no more value to them, until this day.

Tommy wondered if Rossen was going to come. The Viet sharpshooter seemed positive about it. And if Rossen did show, were they going to let him live or just kill him once Rossen was on the ground? He would have no value to them at all that he could see. He was expendable. . . .

Ngu gathered his men to him. "Listen to me and obey!"

They knelt around him. Each had his eyes on him. He was the nearest thing to a living god that they knew. He was the master and they were privileged to serve him.

"Soon the American, Phü Nhãm, will be here. If he brings his security team with him, they will only serve to hinder him. They are yours; kill them when and where you can. But no one is to aim for the Phü Nhãm. He is mine, and mine alone. If he comes alone, then we shall have a hunt and you shall be my beaters to bring him to me." Ngu laughed pleasantly. "Once more we shall have a tiger hunt, but this time it shall be held beneath the Tiger's Breath."

He dismissed them and gave his equipment one last check. His HTl had fresh batteries in it and the Dragunov was in perfect condition; his ammunition had been hand-loaded to his exact specifications and tested. He could give a two-inch shot group at five hundred meters consistently. Here, though, it was unlikely that such a range would be

used. There was too much cover and not a
great deal of open ground. This would be a
stalker's game. For this occasion he went to
the river and cleansed his body, washing
away the dust of the day to be fresh and
pure. He changed from his khakis into a
camouflage uniform, one of the French Foreign Legion's splinter patterns, which would
go well with the differing terrains that the
valley had to offer.

When he was finished with his ablutions,
he passed by Tomanaga in the small clearing where he had him staked out like a goat
to attract the tiger.

Tomanaga called to him, "Hey, shooter!"

Ngu was pleased at the appellation, *shooter*.
It had a pleasing quality to it. He checked
his watch. He had a few minutes left.

"What do you want?"

Tomanaga flexed his back where the muscles were already beginning to cramp and
burn.

"I just wanted to talk to you for a second.
After all, this may be my last chance to talk
to anyone."

Ngu bobbed his head in agreement. "That
is true. This day may very well be your last,
and then again, it may not."

"Where did you learn to speak English so
good?"

Ngu knelt in front of Tomanaga to draw circles in the dirt with a stick. He looked up. "I have always had a gift for languages and made it a point to learn English as perfectly as I could. It comes in handy for listening in to your radio communications. I even tended bar at the American Officers' Club in Nha Trang for a time."

Tomanaga grinned. "I thought you looked familiar, but then all of us gooks look alike."

Ngu broke into open laughter. "That is good, very good. Now I wish that I had spent more time with you. You have kept your courage and your sense of humor. That is a rare quality for one in your precarious position."

Tomanaga rubbed his head against the back of the pole. Lice were building homes in his hair. "What do you think your chances are, if Rossen shows up?"

Ngu rose to his feet and pointed the stick in his hand at Tomanaga. "I will win! You may rest assured on that matter."

"Why are you so confident that you can take Rossen out? He's one of the best in the business."

Ngu tossed the stick away. "True. He is one of the best. But I am *the* best and I have prepared myself *and* him for the coming event." He checked his watch again. "I am sorry to break our conversation off, but as you know, I have a previous engagement and there are still a couple of things to take care of. So, if you will excuse me, I will see you later."

"Want to bet on that?"

Ngu halted in his tracks. There was a note of absolute confidence in the Japanese's voice that he did not like. For him, in his condition, to have such faith that his friend would win was unsettling. He ignored the question. He could not let such things weigh on his mind. He needed to compose himself. He walked away to where his security team was sitting around the small camp fire.

Tomanaga called after him, yelling louder. "Want to bet on that, you Dink son-of-a-bitch?"

Ngu felt his face flush as anger began to build. Then he stopped and laughed, calling back to his prisoner. "That was very good. You almost made me loose my temper. I know what you are trying to do. You want to get me irritated so that I will not think clearly and make mistakes. That will not happen. But, as you say, it was a good try."

Tomanaga spat a hunk of phlegm from his throat. "It's not a try, just a fact. Rossen is going to burn you today."

Ngu had taken just about enough from his captive. He pointed his finger at him.

"If you say just one more word, it will be you who shall burn, and I mean right now. I will have my men build a fire around you and burn you alive for our smoke signal."

Tomanaga shut up. He knew that Ngu meant exactly what he was saying, but he'd accomplished what he wanted anyway. Maybe his words would get under the bastard's skin a bit and take away some of that overbearing confidence and ego.

Ngu ordered his men to go to the face of the falls, climb halfway up the side of the mountain, and set fire to the stack of wood there that had been prepared since the morning.

"Don't forget, at exactly ten minutes to noon set the fire and pour oil on it so our guest will have a good signal. Then you come back to me at once."

He tried to relax with a fresh cup of tea, but that didn't help; he was still angry and even more angry at himself, for he felt that somehow the Japanese had won something and he didn't like that very much. He was used to being the winner in every contest. He threw the rest of the tea into the fire, then poured the pot of water over the coals to put them out.

He was becoming a bit impatient for things to get started. Looking up at the skies, he saw the oily, thick tendril of smoke from the fire set by his men climb into the clean air in a dark, thick column.

He spoke to the sky.

"Come to me, Phü Nhăm; do not disappoint me. Come to me."

CHAPTER SIXTEEN

It was cool on the flight line. In the highlands, the heat of the day didn't usually show up till after pak time. Rossen had made one stop at the PX when it opened and picked up an item he thought he might need later. In his kit he also took some medical supplies, antibiotics and dressings and pain killers. He didn't know what kind of shape Tommy was going to be in. He put the medical kit in a separate pack. Other than that, he was traveling light. Five full magazines, his bayonet, two grenades as usual, and a couple of rations.

Lieutenant Sam Benson was waiting for him. Taking his time, he walked over to the Huey and handed his gear up to the door gunner, who nodded at him. Sam climbed in and told his co-pilot to give Rossen his seat in the nose. Sam's crew knew he was taking a short side trip, but things like that happened and they didn't want to know why. If anything went wrong, then it was his responsibility. *Cover your own ass*, that was the first law of survival. They lifted off. No one had paid any attention to Sam's passenger. One of the things about the army was that if you looked like you knew what you were doing, it wasn't very likely anyone would ever question you.

Once they were clear of the field, Sam asked Rossen, "How are you going to get back out if you do win and get Tommy back?"

"I guess I'll have to walk out, won't I? There's not many buses running up there."

Sam fumed, "Don't always be such a goddamned hard-ass, Rossen. Even if you don't like anybody, Tommy's got a few friends. You get down there and don't get yourself killed, and I'll come back and get you even if Tommy's not with you!"

He instantly regretted the remark about not having any friends. If what Rossen was going to do wasn't for friendship, then he didn't know what it was.

"I'm sorry about that crack I made about

not having any friends, Rossen. I didn't mean
it."

Rossen's mouth gave a twitch at the
corner, not quite a smile.

"Yes, you did, Sam. And probably, until
right now, you were right. I do have a friend
and he's down there and I'm going to get
him back or I'm not coming back."

Sam looked straight ahead toward their
destination.

"You got another one right here, if you
want him."

Rossen felt warm. A good warm he hadn't
known in years.

"Thanks, Sam. I do."

They rode in silence the rest of the way.
Sam knew Rossen had some heavy thinking
to do. Beneath them the mountains ran forever in an endless wave of green, flowing to
the far horizons and beyond. A fantastically
beautiful country to be so deadly. He checked
his map and compass, made a four-degree
turn to the starboard. He broke the silence
by saying to Rossen, "There's your marker."
Straight ahead was a column of smoke. The
comment wasn't necessary; Rossen had already seen it.

"You better go in the rear now and get
ready. Tell my co-pilot to come on up. I
may have to pull out of there in a hurry.
Even as bad as they want you, a chopper's

still quite a prize. That Dink down there might just get greedy."

He passed through the column of oily smoke and began to make his pass down a valley lined with steep cliffs. The floor was cut by a single silver strand, a branch off the Ay Yun river coming from Laos to South Vietnam. In the valley, where the shadows were longer, the green was nearer that of deep turquoise. Ten regiments could have been hidden in one square mile, resting safe, unseen, beneath the lush, green canopy.

Sam wasn't terribly fond of the idea of having to bring Rossen into forbidden territory. If anything happened to the chopper, no one would ever know. No one would ever come to look for him. Even if he got back okay, he'd have a hard time explaining where he'd been and why he'd been out of radio contact for over an hour. But he'd figure out something to tell them. If they didn't like it, they could always send him Stateside as a punishment.

Rossen came back up to stand where he could look straight ahead. Sam pointed through the plexiglass to the valley. "There it is, Sarge. Where do you want to get off at?"

Rossen looked for the landmark and found it. On the southeast wall of the valley, a narrow waterfall dropped off the edge of the plateau, falling over five hundred feet to the river below.

"There, at the base of the waterfall. Make one pass up and back down the valley so I can get a look; then take me in as low as you can. Drop me off and then you get your ass out of here. Like you said, this bird of yours is too tempting a target."

Sam agreed with everything. He made one quick run down the valley and back. From the sky, nothing could be seen. Near the base of the waterfall, where mist rose in foaming clouds, he brought the chopper in until he hovered less than three feet off the bank.

Rossen didn't waste any time thanking him. Grabbing his gear, he leaped the few feet to the soft spongy bank and moved into the trees out of sight without looking back.

Sam was clear of the ridge before Rossen had time to settle down and take a close look at the hunting grounds. From the air, it was more like a bed of moss; from the earth, it was a forest primeval. Giant trees reached to the heavens. The upper branches clustered together, each trying to get its share of the sun. This was an old forest, not much new growth—there wasn't light enough for new trees to grow, only for patches of brush, ferns and parasitic vines that dangled from the limbs of the trees or were wrapped in tendrils as thick as a man's thighs around their trunks, where they slowly squeezed the tree to death, then used its corpse to rise higher toward the light.

Taking cover low to the earth where he could see down the river for about two hundred meters, he waited, letting his senses take in everything—the smell, the colors. There wasn't much sound here. The roar of the waterfall muted the air.

Well, time to check in. If Ngu is here, then he'd know I am too. Staying in the prone position, he took the radio out of his butt pack and switched it on, adjusting the squelch.

"You there, Ngu?"

The walkie-talkie immediately barked back. "Right here, Phü Nhām. I'm glad you got here all right. What I want you to do now is come down the river on the bank about a kilometer and you'll see your friend. Then we'll do what we have to."

Rossen clicked his talk button. "How do I know that he's still alive?"

"How do you say it? No sweat, GI. I'll show you." There were a few moments of silence; then Rossen wished he hadn't asked, as a long, ululating scream came over the small radio. There were no words, but Rossen knew it was Tomanaga.

As quickly as it had begun, the scream ended, was cut off abruptly.

"By the way, that was not an act of random cruelty. Your friend was just being chastised for something he said earlier. Do you have any further questions, Phü Nhām?"

The HTl was shaking in his hand. The little bastard was beginning to get to him, and knowing that pissed him off even more. "No, you little shit. That's all. You just stay where you are. It's going to be a pleasure to let you hold one right between your yellow slit eyes, you motherfucker."

Ngu laughed pleasantly at Rossen's response. He knew that he was having the desired effect. If Rossen stayed mad, then he'd have a better chance of making mistakes.

Keeping to the cover of the river bank, he moved upriver. He knew that Ngu could be lying in wait for him, but he didn't think so. Ngu had too much ego; he wouldn't want the game he was playing to end that fast. He hadn't finished talking.

Letting his instincts take over, he tried to clear his mind as he moved along the bank, stopping every few steps to listen, see, feel. The mist from the waterfall was left behind.

Overhead, the sun was nearing its zenith. He wanted to hurry, to get to Tomanaga, but knew that he couldn't take one wrong step; a hurried action could be his last, especially if he had misjudged Ngu and the little bastard was laying for him. He knew the Viet had the advantage of being familiar with the terrain, and if it had been him, he would have been set up to make his hit as soon as his quarry hit the deck from the chopper. If he had any advantage, that was it. Ngu wanted to play, and he wanted to kill.

Ngu had everything ready. He was sure that the next item on his psy-war program would drive Rossen over the brink to where he'd do something stupid. This was even better than he'd thought it would be. The excitement level was higher than anything he'd ever experienced.

Time to bait his quarry a bit more. He pushed his talk button. "How are you doing there, Sergeant? What's taking you so long? Don't you trust me? I promise you that I will keep my word. There is no one here but you and me. Oh, and of course, your friend, the Japanese. Kill me and he is yours."

Rossen's response took a lot of the wind out of Ngu's sails. "Don't worry, I'm coming, but listen to me. If anything happens to Tomanaga, if you try to pull any shit or hurt him any more, I'm going to turn around and leave. Then you can go and play with yourself."

Ngu was shocked! Now he had to make his decision. Was he bluffing or would Rossen do as he threatened and pull out? He couldn't let that happen, even if it did mess up some of his plans a bit.

"Don't worry, Sergeant. I will live up to my end of our bargain. Call me when you see your friend."

Rossen clicked off the radio. He didn't want a call from Ngu giving his position away. It took another five minutes before Rossen could make out Tommy tied to the stake. In the scope, he could see he was alive but couldn't tell how badly hurt he was. Well, the only way he was going to know was to get Ngu's game started.

He slid back and began to move around the clearing where Tommy was held. Rossen moved slowly, taking his time. This was where all the woodcraft and years of hunting experience would be needed. A shadow crossed the bole of a banana palm. Through the ART, he could just make out a hand and knee. Whoever it was, he was now standing right behind the plant.

He checked to his left, right and rear, but he could neither see nor hear anything. Setting his sight waist-high on the soft-bodied banana palm, he fired three quick shots, each a few inches higher than the previous one. The man behind the tree was blown off his feet, knocked seven feet away, with two of the three rounds connecting. One down!

He rolled to his side and onto his knees and half-crawled away. This was no good! There was too much cover here for him to have any real chance. The odds were that he'd just stumble over someone who'd see him first and get blown away. He needed a better place to work. Make them come to him.

He headed for the side of the mountain. When they'd flown over, Rossen had seen some spots where he'd have a good field of fire and some cover, but it wasn't so thick that they could just walk up on him. He gave himself a five-minute headstart and was just beginning to climb up when he decided he better give Ngu a call. Switching his radio back on, he called softly, "You there, Ngu?"

"*Xa phai*, yes, I am here. It seems that first blood is yours. But it's the last blood that counts."

Rossen scoped out the area below. He was about a hundred feet above the valley floor. Ngu was probably near the clearing with Tommy. He couldn't see anything. Better let them know I'm around. He shook a middle-sized, grey, round rock loose with his feet and rolled it down the hill. The sound should bring them running to get a fix on him.

He climbed.

"He is going up the side of the mountain," Ngu cried to the three remaining men. "Spread out and get above him if you can. Make noises; let him know where you are. Then run him back to me. I'll be in the center!" They ran to obey.

Resting his back against a clump of boulders, Rossen scanned the area. To his left he saw one of Ngu's men trying to get a grip on a cluster of vines to pull himself up on some rocks.

Rossen let him hold one. This was too easy. They should know better. Why was Ngu just throwing his men away? Then it hit him. They were expendable and were just being used to keep a fix on him. Ngu didn't care if they got killed. Well, now, if that's how he wants it, then I'll glad to oblige him. He moved on a bit higher above the cluster of boulders. He stopped for a few minutes, his eyes taking in everything around him. Then he moved on to the right. If they were trying to flank him, then there would probably be more over there. He dropped to his knees in a clump of tall, yellow grass. He was right! There was another one. He brought him under fire, hitting the man right above his left ear, turning the skull into pulp. A sonic crack by his own head made him drop and roll into a bamboo thicket. There was another one and he'd almost gotten smoked!

He rolled back downhill, hit a patch of loose gravel on a steep slope, and slid seventy feet before he could stop. Above him he heard a man cry out, and knew it was another man on Ngu's team telling his boss where he was. Turning onto his back to dig his heels in where he could get some traction, he saw a tiny figure at the bottom of the hill, about eight hundred meters away. He tried to move out, but just stayed more or less in place, his heels not finding anything to get a hold on.

He knew that he was in the Viet's scope. A hammer hit his right thigh, knocking him loose. He slid down the rocks another thirty feet, until he could catch himself by grabbing onto the trunks of a couple of small trees. Using them, he turned back over onto his stomach and rolled away from the slide area into a larger growth of old bamboo the thickness of his biceps.

Goddamn, that son-of-a-bitch can shoot. The round hadn't gone all the way through; it was still lodged in his thigh and burning like hell.

That's going to slow me down a lot. I've got to do something else! Taking valuable seconds to tie on a battle dressing to the outside of his bloody trouser leg, he moved around, careful to stay out of sight, heading back to the boulders.

He crawled into the rock field, knowing that he'd left some spoor on the way. Head swimming, he resisted the temptation to take one of the pain pills. At least pain would keep him alert. Scoping out the way he had come, he saw a small movement in the trees just off to his right. There was a clear area on both sides of the boulders for about twenty or thirty meters. The movement came again. He scoped on it. He could make out the head of a man crawling on his belly straight toward him.

Rossen zeroed right on the top of the Viet's head when he paused and put the side of his face to earth to catch a breath. The M14 bucked against his shoulder; the bullet hit the Viet dead-center in the top of his skull and passed straight into his chest, through the throat, into the lungs and finally the abdomen, where it exited just to the left of his spine, right above the tail bone.

Now Rossen went to work. He had lot to do in the next minutes!

Rossen's M14 cracked. Ngu now had a sound and, he thought, possibly a sight fix. Adjusting his focus, he had no luck. A little movement in some brush in and around a cluster of boulders. The boulders presented several places which would be a good shooting site, though. He had checked them out in his earlier reconnaissance of the valley. It was very possible that was where Rossen was holed up. The blood spoor was going in that general direction, until he lost it. . . .

His radio crackled at his hip.

"Are you calling me, Phü Nhãm? Over."

"Yeah, why don't you come on up and get me? You know you hit me and I can't get around so good. So if we're going to ever end this thing, you're going to have to do the walking.

By the way, I think I nailed your last man . . . that is, unless you have any more with you?"

"No, Phü Nhãm, that was all. And they

have served their purpose. Now it is between us."

"Good, then you come on up and visit for a while." Ngu did not like that very much. He knew as well as Rossen that one firing from a fixed position had certain advantages and that in the art of cover-and-concealment, movement was the most dangerous course of action. But if Rossen was hit, then it was necessary for him to go up and finish the kill. He was not, however, in any great hurry. He settled back to wait a while, to let time and pain take their toll on the American. After another hour-and-a-half passed, Rossen called him again.

The radio crackled incessantly. "Come on up, you gook son-of-a-bitch. I can't go down after you. What's the matter, afraid of me? Can't figure out where I am? Here, I'll help you." Another shot from the M14 and Ngu was sure that Rossen was in, or very near, the boulders. But was this a trap of some kind?

"Come on, Ngu. Do I have to spell things out for you? Tell you what, you've got your radio. When you think you're getting near to me, I'll start doing a count for you. You can tell if you're getting close by the volume. How's that? Anything else I can do for you, chicken-shit?"

Ngu bit his tongue to keep control of his words.

"You will not have to do anything more. I am coming."

"Better hurry, then. It'll be dark in a couple of hours. So you better get me while there's still some light. It's dangerous to walk around these mountains in the dark."

Ngu had already started up the side of the mountain, but not taking the direct route. He angled over so that he would pass the cluster of boulders to his right by some distance, go above them, then come down behind them. He wondered if Rossen was actually going to do a count. Maybe he had lost enough blood that he was not thinking straight. Many possibilities, all of them very dangerous to take for granted.

He did not break cover as he climbed. He still thought Rossen was in or near the cluster of boulders and kept to where he was out of sight line from them. Several times he paused and took a look. At each pause he spoke over his radio.

"Are you still there, Phü Nhām?" And each time Rossen answered him. "Yes! Are you ready for your count?"

Ngu would go silent again and climb higher. At last he was where he wanted to be. Through his scope he could make out the rear of the cluster of boulders. There was something different about them than when he'd been up here before. What was it? Slowly, working as carefully as a pathologist examining a culture under his microscope, Ngu scoped it out. He laughed silently. He had it. . . . There was more cover around one section of the boulders than there had been earlier, and several of the soft-bodied plants used in the cover had already begun to wilt.

Now to find out if Rossen was there or if this was some kind of ambush. He spoke into the radio very softly. "Phű Nhām, are you there?"

"Where the hell did you expect me to be—Miami?"

"You can begin your count now, Phű Nhām. It is time."

"What are you whispering for? Are you that close? Well, it doesn't make any difference. The bone's broke in my leg and I can't move. So come on up. Here's your count.

"One!"

Ngu could hardly believe it. The American *was* going to count for him. But he had something else in mind rather than using his radio for any kind of fix. He would use his own ears when he neared the boulders. If he did not hear Rossen counting there, then he would know it was a trap.

"Two."

Ngu began his descent, moving as carefully as he ever had before, taking advantage of every inch of cover. When he stopped and tried to get a sight picture on the blind, he had no luck; the cover was too thick.

"Thirty ... come on, Ngu, I'm getting tired."

Rossen kept counting and talking, usually having something insulting to say. Ngu was now less than twenty meters from the boulders and stopped, let his heartbeat slow down so it wouldn't pound in his ears. He listened without his radio.

"Seventy–five. You going to take all day, Dink?"

He could hear the count with his own ears, and it was coming from the boulders. Perhaps Rossen was bleeding to death and this bravado and vulgar speech of his was only the last frustrated act of one who has really given up the fight.

Ngu focused on the boulders again. He couldn't see Rossen, but there was a glint of light reflecting off something. Perhaps the gun barrel? Something was near a cleft in the rocks.

"Eighty. For God's sake, aren't you ever going to get here?"

Ngu promised himself and Rossen that he would indeed get there and it would be soon. The count below became louder and clearer as Ngu crept forward. In his mind he was now the tiger stalking his wounded prey in the rocks. This was delicious!

"Ninety–two, and I'm still here. Where are you, little man?"

Ngu was very close now, sliding silent as a delta cobra over the last barrier of boulders between him and the blind. He paused. He didn't need the scope; it was too close for that. He was less than ten meters away. There was a heavy blood sign leading right into the blind. With his naked eye, from thirty feet away, he could see the form of his quarry through holes in the cover. He could see the broken outline of a head with a camouflage cap on it. Grass for camouflage was stuck in a band around it and on his back and neck where he leaned forward. The rest of his body was concealed by the cover, but he could make out the tip of the American's rifle barrel resting between a crack in the boulders and aimed downhill. And he could still hear him counting and teasing. Good enough, he would tease no more.

"One hundred and one. Damn it, are you going to take forever?"

At this range, for one such as he, there was no need to put the Dragunov to his shoulder. He rose to his feet and fired from the hip, putting round after round into the shadowy form. He saw the American's body shake and shudder with each bullet and his rifle go falling to the hillside below.

His heart pounding with passion, he fired off every round in his magazine into the blind, knowing that his bullets were hitting. There would be no more talk from the so-called *Phü Nhäm*, the famous Ice Man. Ngu cried out, "No! You do not have to wait anymore. I am here!"

He lowered his rifle to his side, emotionally exhausted, and started to walk toward his victim.

"I am too, Dink!"

Ngu whirled around in time to see Rossen standing behind him, bare-chested, a thick-bladed knife in his hand, moving forward. Rossen's bayonet sank to the hilt in Ngu's stomach, edge-up. Rossen slapped Ngu's empty rifle from his hand and grabbed the Vietnamese by the shoulder and pulled him close to him as he slid the razor edge of his blade up, splitting Ngu from his navel to his sternum. Then he stepped back. Ngu stood there, eyes already fogging, mind bewildered. How could the American have been behind him when he had heard him talking to the front?

"How?"

He slid to his knees. Rossen gave him his answer. "A portable tape recorder with a tape I made this morning. A rubber band on the HT's talk button and there you have it. Not so tough to figure out now, was it? I looked this area over pretty good and knew the only way you could get to me here was from the top down."

Ngu tried to keep his intestines from falling out onto the ground. He fell forward to his face, his mouth sucking puffs of dust from the earth, then blowing them out again.

Rossen leaned over. "You were too confident, Comrade; that made you impatient. You were playing a game. And you couldn't stop thinking you had to do it with a rifle. Dumb shit! You never thought about knives. You just wanted to play and I came here to kill. So good night and say hello to your ancestors for me." He placed the edged tip of his bayonet under Ngu's throat where it touched the small hollow under his left ear, stretched Ngu's head back by pulling at a handful of hair, and cut deep and steady. From ear to ear. He was surprised that there wasn't more blood, but maybe the gut wound had caused most of Ngu's fluids to drain into his abdominal cavity. He let the half-severed head drop. This was over.

*   *   *

He went into the blind, moving the decoy he had made of his jacket aside. The jacket had been stuffed with twigs and grass, and the head was just a large gourd he'd picked up from a patch of them growing on vines between the boulders. He put the jacket back on; even with all the bullet holes in it, it was better than nothing. He put the HT1 and the small Sony tape recorder into his side pants pocket and buttoned down the flap. He wouldn't need them anymore for a time. He went back down the hillside. Going around to the front, he picked up his rifle. The scope had been smashed in the fall, but the rest of it was okay. By the time he reached Tomanaga, there was less than an hour of light left.

Tomanaga's head had dropped. His arms and legs were swollen from the hours of standing. When he felt his bonds being cut and gentle hands easing him to the earth from the post, he knew.

"Rossen" he croaked, "you son-of-a-bitch. I told Ngu you'd take him."

Giving Tomanaga some water, Rossen helped him back to his feet.

"We got to go. There's still one more mountain to climb." Together, they climbed back up the mountainside, this time taking a good trail and knowing there would be no one on it to stop them. By the time they reached the crest near where the waterfall began, the sun was turning the plateau into a rich blending of reds and oranges mixed with the yellow grass and green of the foliage.

Tomanaga rested his back against a tall, thinly barked tree. "How are we going to get out of here?"

Rossen looked to the sky. Coming from the south, a huge dragonfly was heading their way.

"Don't worry about it. We have a friend coming to give us a ride."

Tomanaga didn't know what had happened, but for some reason the "Ice Man" had begun to melt a little. He closed his eyes to wait.